A Century of Supernatural Stories

A Century of Supernatural Stories

Richard Sugg

For Emily

CONTENTS

Poltergeists

Ghosts

Vampires

Fairies

Witches

Unnatural Animals

Magic

Corpse Magic

Apparitions

The Evil Eye

Religion

The Unexplained and the Uncategorisable...

A Century of Stories: (I) The Supernatural

I am very lucky: I love stories, and I love history, and stories and history are the bulk of my job. What is it about these stories in particular? I have chosen the ones here for several reasons. Sometimes, there is a lot of exact detail to bring an otherwise incredible incident close up to us, to make it more real than shorter, more abstract tales. Where we have only few details (and occasionally not a single person's name) I have included a story because in just a handful of lines we are yet presented with a picture and a state of mind that, without that record, we could simply *never have imagined for ourselves* (the Paddington chapel vault is one example of this).

One other big element of these tales is what they tell us about the vast gulf between the minds of the poor and the privileged, the illiterate and the educated, during the nineteenth century. As you will see below, the richer and more learned minority were frequently staggered when they came up against beliefs about witch-craft, fairies, ghosts, and magic in general. At times they seem genuinely unable to fully believe the evidence of their own ears or eyes. At others, they seem indignant; at others, again, perhaps even faintly guilty that they lead a society which allows
these apparently insane beliefs to flourish. And yet, in fairness to certain of the élite, they did also attempt, sometimes, to acknowledge such beliefs in a very hard-headed, very serious

way: namely, in the courts of law which often saw people accused of crimes inspired by superstition. The Hammersmith Ghost; the Bridget Cleary Changeling Murder; and even the more obscure 1822 cutting of a witch in Somerset all show magical beliefs affecting or moulding the law.

Why the nineteenth century? One reason is that there were now so many more papers, journals and magazines – and, accordingly, so many more stories. Of course, there are more still in the twentieth century, with changes in communication and literacy, and more still now, some two decades into the age of the internet. But it is in the nineteenth century that we get such a fine balance of quantity and quality: stories with pace, shape, and (above all) some unforgettable details.

Perhaps, if I was forced to choose just one thing about these stories which compels me most, it would be this: here, wrenched out of the shadows of humble cottages or slums, is *real history*. It is what people actually believed about the world. To put this another way: imagine, for a moment, that you have almost no belongings, that you cannot write, and that there are no photographs of you. When you die, what would be left? This was the position most people were in for much of history. But these stories, especially once we begin to understand their details, and to connect them to similar tales, let us inside the heads and the lives of those dead, crumbled, anonymous people.

Where possible, I have let these stories speak for themselves. Where the details can be obscure or ambiguous, I've spoken up briefly to offer glosses or interpretations, as well as some comparisons with other such cases. I hope I've got the balance about right.

At times it seems to me that there is no end to the random, extraordinary kaleidoscope of tales that flutters up off these pages from the presses of the Regency and Victorian eras. The excitement and the wonder they inspire is almost impossible to describe – a sensation of falling into the past, bouncing from one point to another of this great net of human tales and oddities and horrors, and never reaching the floor. Welcome, then, to the *Century of Stories* – there is probably no end to them, and you need to bring nothing with you, save your imagination.

Poltergeists

Much of what we encounter here shows us that most people, from the days of Byron through to Wilde, were immensely superstitious. They were terrified witless by tricks, by unseen birds or animals – sometimes even just the rattling of a poker at night in the nextdoor grate. The general motto seems to have been: "if in doubt, assume a ghost". Little wonder that nineteenth-century journalists readily took the opposite stance, after seeing so much hysteria with so little supernatural foundation. Their motto was frequently: "if in doubt, assume natural causes". But in the case of poltergeists, they were wrong. Poltergeists are clearly real. Or, rather: the set of bizarre effects (rappings, objects floated or hurled by no visible cause, unexplained fires – to name a very few) clustered under that name are clearly real. I strongly suspected this myself, after a few weeks reading of well-documented cases – and was sharply convinced when friends, confronted with the subject, then responded: "yes – that's happened to me".

To clarify: despite the name (German for 'racketing or noisy ghost') poltergeists may or may not involve otherworldly agency. At the simplest level, almost all cases (I have collected around 500) centre very clearly on one person

– the 'poltergeist agent' is usually someone between the ages of 10-20, and usually someone who is emotionally troubled in some way. Unable to release or express these traumas in an adequate conscious manner, they unconsciously vent their frustrations through poltergeist events. The most obvious feature of these cases is therefore 'Haunted People', rather than 'Haunted Houses'. Hence the way that, when a family tries to escape by fleeing their home, the events will simply follow them, when the agent moves too.

I would like to be able to give a clear general opinion on the big central question: ghost or no ghost? I in fact started off fairly confident that poltergeist cases were all purely human affairs. But the more evidence you see, the harder it becomes to deny the very strong possibility that a sizeable number of poltergeist incidents do involve a ghost. Indeed: for me perhaps the biggest personal experience of this research has been realising that ghosts do exist. What they are and what they mean are more difficult questions to answer.

One other brief word on poltergeist events. Why do they get the first chapter? I have to admit it was a tough fight for that position, between ghost and poltergeist. But (apart from the fact that, with poltergeist and ghost in boxing ring, the one hurling a storm of crockery and stones is really bound to win) we plunge in at the deep end with these weirdest of entities just because they do offer us a general skeleton key to so many other supernatural phenomena. Most of the supposed ghosts, witches, fairies or black magic feared by these people were nothing of the sort. But poltergeist events clearly *have* been involved in what were thought to be supernatural incidents. Basically, if people are afraid enough of something, they can at times generate poltergeist phenomena. This has happened in supposed vampire episodes; witchcraft cases; and ghost ones. (In many nineteenth century cases, in fact, 'ghost' effectively just means 'poltergeist'). Surprisingly enough, it has also sometimes occurred amongst people who are afraid of fairies (as can be seen in the case described by Shirley Hibbert). Much more on this rich and wonderful topic elsewhere.

1. An Unchivalrous Ghost

The Morning Post, 27 January 1804.

'A singular occurrence has recently taken place at Mytton Old Hall, near Boroughbridge, Yorkshire. This house had for a considerable time been untenanted, owing to a rumour generally circulated, in that part of the country, that it was haunted. About a year since, a very respectable family, despising such ridiculous notions, entered upon the premises, which they inhabited for some time undisturbed. The particular room which had been pointed out was used as the bedroom of one of the tenant's daughters, and a young lady then on a visit to her. Strange noises were occasionally heard, and being generally attributed to a servant, he was discharged upon suspicion.

However, about the middle of last November, the two young ladies were awakened by what they thought was the snapping of a pistol by their bed-side. They listened for some time with considerable anxiety and alarm, scarcely daring to breathe; when at last, by an invisible power, they were forced out of the bed and room, with so much violence, that the noise was distinctly heard over the whole house. In consequence of this extraordinary event, every possible search was made, and "those felt doubts, who ne'er felt doubts before". The respectability of the family, and the acknowledged veracity of the terrified females, induced many confident visitors, clergymen, and others, to examine into the cause of such strange occurrences. Clergymen have slept in the room, and others have watched throughout the whole night, but all experienced similar disturbances, with more or less violence, and have quitted the house in silent thought and reflection, upon the origin of what they now uniformly believe to be the work of no human means. The family are now leaving the residence, which they can no longer tenant with domestic comfort. At a future period the artificer will no doubt be detected, and we trust the contrivers of so mischievous a device will not escape unpunished.'

We will meet something remarkably like that 'snapping of a pistol' below, upon a haunted ship, the H.M.S. Asp, some decades later. The force with which the girls are bundled, not just out of bed, but out of the room is impressive, though not unknown. Some readers may have seen, in May 2015, Sky's dramatised version of the Enfield Poltergeist. During this long drawn out poltergeist case, Janet and her sister Rose were frequently flipped out of bed (as, incidentally, was my old Sociology teacher, Mike, during a poltergeist incident in his house in the 1960s.) And at one point Janet was dragged violently downstairs.

It is very hard to believe that Mytton Hall was the hoax the reporter claims. As so often, with a 'respectable' nineteenth-century family involved, the journalist must assume they themselves are not lying (in our own time, to be fair, we tend to take the same attitude if the witnesses involved are 'educated'). This class bias indeed extends nicely to the clearly unjust sacking of the male servant. His dismissal was one of many cases in which servants were blamed for poltergeist events, and officially harassed, or covertly bullied. So... how did the hoaxer do this, not once but several times, to various clergymen and other 'confident' (presumably, 'sceptical') visitors? And who was the hoaxer? It would have been a brave servant indeed who tried this after one of their number had been promptly sacked for supposedly doing the same a few weeks back. As in other such cases, my attitude here is that I would like to see the 'hoax' repeated successfully, using the available technology of 1803.

Mytton Old Hall is now Mitton Hall Hotel, so if you ever stay or visit you can use your imagination to see how its older sections (dating back to the fifteenth century) lend themselves very well to a good English haunting. Failing that, do have a look at J.M.W. Turner's picture of the Great Hall, c.1799. If I was a ghost, I'd eat in there every night.

2. The Tower of London Ghost
The Royal Cornwall Gazette, 20 January 1816.

'For some weeks past, a family residing in the Tower of London have been very much annoyed and disturbed by a variety of unpleasant and strange noises heard in different parts of the house, during the night; and the sentries on duty at the door of the Royal Regalia, to which this house belongs, have frequently been disturbed by the most violent knocking, and (according to their account) even deep and hollow groans have been heard; and the feeling of superstition having spread very much among the soldiery, with whom the ghost is now a cant phrase, an additional sentry has lately been placed on the rampart immediately over the mysterious spot, and every possible exertion used by the occupier of the house, towards elucidating the cause of the disturbance.

Officers of the garrison have watched for whole nights; nothing but a continuance of the noise was heard, but no visible cause discovered, until, late on the night of Thursday last, the inhabitants of the Tower were thrown into the greatest possible confusion, by the screaming and roaring of the sentry stationed at the door of the Regalia depot, and the turning out of the guard, which, upon repairing to the spot, found the soldier extended on the pavement in a senseless state. He was immediately carried off to the guard room, and when sufficiently restored to his senses, positively affirmed that whilst upon duty a small figure crept from under the door at which he was stationed, and gradually made its approach to him, at the same time changing its appearance to that of a human being, and afterwards into that of a dog. These sudden transformations so completely affrighted the solider, that after alarming the neighbourhood with his bellowing, he fell down senseless.

Nothing was seen by the soldier placed on the rampart, and the most rational conclusion is, that imbecility of mind, has in this case been worked upon by the ridiculous and absurd tales of the ghost, with which, most probably, the poor fellow's weak brains have been crammed; and certainly no rational person can say that doubling the sentries for such reasons as in this case, tends much to assure the uneducated mind of such fallacies, as it appears this soldier has fallen a martyr to.

At the same time it is absolutely necessary that proper methods should be resorted to, to clear up the mystery with which it is at present enveloped; although there is very little doubt but that in a building so ancient as the one in question, containing numerous passages and blocked-up apartments, loop-holes, and crevices, Boreas occasionally gives a concert, in which he is most musically accompanied by all the bats, and consequently many cats of the garrison'.

The Morning Post, 29 January 1816.

'The soldier who was so much frightened by the supposed ghost in the Tower, we regret to state, is since dead!'.

3. The Bell-Ringing Ghost
The Belfast News-Letter, 4 February 1831; citing *Aberdeen Observer* 28 Jan.

'For two or three weeks past, the family of the Rev. Mr Browning had been subjected to a very novel species of annoyance – the bells in the house were violently rung without any assignable cause; and every method adopted to discover the agent that was employed proved abortive. As the bells were always silent during the night, suspicion fell upon the servants. They were questioned separately, when the youngest [servant] girl declared that she had several times seen Mary Wilson, her fellow servant, taking down her hand, with a hearth brush in it, from under the bells, the moment they had been set a-ringing. Mary Wilson was accordingly charged with the offence, and, after some hesitation, she confessed her guilt.

Mr Browning, conceiving that the matter ought not to be passed over in silence, applied to the Procurator-Fiscal, who directed that the girl supposed ghost in the Tower, we regret to state, is should be summoned before the Magistrates, and she was accordingly placed at the bar. A number of witnesses were examined. It appeared, that besides the ringing of the bells, now and then a plate or other article would be dashed upon the floor, and then several of the cooking vessels would share the same fate; in short, to such a height did the disturbance arrive, that a report went abroad that the house was haunted. Mary Wilson, being examined by the Court ... declared that she was innocent of ringing the bells, except on two occasions, when she had done it *in fun.* This was only a week ago, and the bells had been ringing for two weeks before.

The little girl [ie, the youngest servant] detailed the ringing of the bells, and the breaking of the crockery, and stated that she herself on two occasions had rung the bells *for fun.* The bells had often rung when Mary was in church, and witness was the only servant in the house. Mary had refused to sleep with her mistress's mother – her mistress found fault with her, and after that the bells began to ring.

A baker, who served Mr Browning with bread, was examined for the defence. He always went into the kitchen with the bread, and sometimes stopped a short time. On one occasion he heard the bells ringing violently, and at another time he saw the tongues of the bells move, when they did not ring, and is certain that on none of these occasions any of the girls were to blame. Other witnesses stated that they had heard the bells ringing when Mary was not in a situation to touch them. The Magistrates expressed their conviction of her guilt, and sentenced her to pay a fine of 20s plus expenses, or to be confined in gaol for 20 days. The fine was paid, and Mary was set at liberty.'

No prizes for noticing that, once again, the humble servant, Mary Wilson, is relatively powerless here. Rev. Browning is determined to believe in a hoax, and so happily listens to the (probably malicious) youngest servant, whilst ignoring the visiting baker. There is in fact an interesting reason why the bells did not ring in the night, and one typical of poltergeist activity. We will come to it shortly, via The Claverham Ghost. The Aberdeen case is partly similar to the famous Bealings Bells: in 1834 at Great Bealings house, near Woodbridge in Suffolk, the servant bells rang repeatedly, with no hoaxer ever detected, despite ferociously careful observation.

One other little detail could easily slip by here, were it not for the sharp eye of your genial host. This is the fact that the bells began to ring *after* the argument which Mary had about sleeping with the old lady. Mary therefore almost certainly became anxious, if not highly nervous. And she was therefore almost certainly the poltergeist agent in this case, unconsciously discharging nervous energy through the bell ringing.

4. The Haunted House at Windsor.

Trewman's Exeter Flying Post, 24 June 1841.

'Windsor is in a ferment on account of some miraculous noises which are daily and nightly heard in a house called Want's Grove, at Clewer. They resemble a rapping of the knuckles on a board, and are audible five hundred yards off. So strong is the witchcraft that a door has once been broken in two, and once forced off its hinges. All the usual excitement is felt on the occasion; people have watched at night; and the house is visited by crowds, including the Magistrates of the place. Meanwhile, all the people in the place are giving notices of quittance to their landlords.'

The Standard, 16 June 1841.

'Windsor, Tuesday. A Haunted House. For some few days past Windsor and its immediate neighbourhood have been in a state of considerable excitement, in consequence of a house known as "Want's Cottage", standing alone, surrounded by its grounds, at Clewer, about a mile from the town, having been reported, from the extraordinary noises which have been heard there, to be "haunted". The house is occupied by Mr and Mrs Wright (who have for some years past retired from business), their two daughters, and a female domestic.

The noises which have been heard, and which are continued at intervals throughout the day and night, resemble those which would be caused by a person rapidly striking his knuckles against the panel of a door for two or three seconds ... several magistrates of the county, clergymen, and the most influential residents of the neighbourhood, have visited the house, the whole of whom have been present during the time the extraordinary noises have been repeated; and, although they have evidently proceeded from a door leading from the kitchen into the water-closet in the house, close to which the parties have stationed themselves, they have been unable to throw the least light upon the affair.

The following magistrates of the county and other gentlemen ... were present during yesterday and a part of Saturday: Mr W.F. Riley, Forest Hill; Mr W.B. Harcourt, St Leonard's Hill; Major General Clement Hill; Mr Edmund Foster, Clewer House; the Rev Mr Gould, of Clewer, etc. The sound clearly proceeds from the door I have described, and can only be in any way imitated, and upon that door only, by striking the knuckles hard and rapidly upon the centre of the panel. Mr Riley and Lord Clement Hill stationed themselves in the hall within three yards of this door, and, as soon as the knocking commenced, rushed to the spot within a second afterwards, but not a soul was near it, and the whole of the family were in a different part of the house. The knocking is so loud that it is heard by the inmates of houses 400 or 500 yards off. Such is the alarm these strange, and, at present unaccountable, noises, have caused throughout the neighbourhood, that a lady named Roberts, who resides some distance from Mr Wright, and whose house is divided from his by two public roads, has given notice to her landlord that she will quit today, and Mr Wright's family [are said to be] ...making preparations to leave the house immediately.

The whole of the machinery of the water closet has been removed, the flooring taken up, and the ground excavated, under the impression that the noise might have proceeded from foul air in the pipes or drains ... but the noise still continues as before, at intervals, and today and yesterday it was even more violent and loud than ever. In order to ascertain if the door of the closet was [actually] struck, a small piece of chip was laid upon the projecting portion of the panel, and after the knocking had ceased, this had fallen on the floor. And on Sunday last ... Mr Wright's son, who had arrived that morning from Newbury, fastened up the door by means of a piece of wire; and, after the noise had ceased, the wire upon examination was found broken, and the door forced inwards. At one time the door was broken off its hinges, and placed at the back of the closet, but the knocking was precisely the same as before.

The landlady of the house (Mrs Stokes) has arrived from town, and has since caused every inquiry to be instituted, but without the least hopes at present of unravelling the extraordinary mystery. It should be observed that at three or four times when the knocking took place there were five persons, and sometimes more, present from Windsor and elsewhere, who were determined, if possible, to detect the cause; and who were totally unconnected with the family residing in the house; but they were still left in ignorance of its origin ... On Saturday last a gentleman volunteered to sit up with Mr Wright during the whole of that night ... The rest of the family retired to rest at the usual hour, and up to six o'clock the next morning no noises were heard, but in the course of Sunday they were more violent than ever. Many ignorant persons, of course, ascribe the noises to some supernatural agency, and a tale is now current that some person left that neighbourhood some time back "in a very mysterious manner" and that "no doubt a murder was committed near the spot". However this may be, gentlemen of high standing in the county ... have visited the house during the past week, and certainly to say the least, they are all exceedingly puzzled at the extraordinary noises they have heard within three or four yards of the spot where they had stationed themselves. This singular affair continues to excite the most intense interest, and to be wrapped in the greatest mystery.'

Aside from the social pedigree of the witnesses, two details are notable here. One is that a noise so loud could probably not be made by a hoaxer, however ingenious they were. (Compare, below, the noise like 'fifty men with mallets' at the house of Mr Traves in 1868). The other is the six o'clock restart for the noises on the Sunday morning. This sounds like just the time when the servant (the very probable agent of the noises) would be obliged to rise for her chores. As will be evident in several of these cases, poltergeist agents very rarely cause trouble when sleeping.

The Times, 26 June 1841.
'The "Haunted" House At Clewer, Near Windsor'.

'The extraordinary knocking (supposed to be against the door of the watercloset) having still continued, with even increased violence, an intelligent man, belonging to the Windsor police, has been stationed on the premises during the past week; and, notwithstanding he has frequently been within two or three yards of the spot whence the sound proceeded, at the very time, he has not been able to make the least discovery of its apparently mysterious origin.

A scientific gentleman, from London, having seen in the papers an account of the noises, has visited the premises three times during the last ten days (the

27

last time was on Monday, at the request of the tenant), and tried various experiments to endeavour to discover the cause, but without the least success. The boards of the floor, both inside and around the closet, have been all taken up, and excavations made to the depth of several feet. The drain has been opened and closely examined, and the party has even gone so far with his experiments as to have the water in an adjoining ditch analysed! Mr Manly, the parish sexton, attended with the gravedigger's sounding iron, and sounded the ground, within and without, to the depth of upwards of five feet, but no clue was obtained, and the knocking still continued at intervals as before. On Monday last the noises were more frequent and violent than ever. The policeman, who was on the alert during the whole day, counted, within twelve hours, thirteen distinct knockings of the same character as have been before described.

On the following day (Tuesday), at twelve o'clock, the family removed from the house, taking with them the whole of their furniture. Previously to their leaving, the knocking came on, at half past 7 o'clock that morning, the policeman being there.

As an extraordinary sensation was created throughout the neighbourhood on the subject, as well as certain suspicions excited, four respectable gentlemen of Windsor were determined to ascertain if the noise had been caused by means of trickery (which was strongly suspected) or not. They, therefore ... agreed to go to the house that evening, and remain there during the whole of the night. They did so, accompanied by the policeman and two other persons who resided in the neighbourhood. From 9 o'clock (the hour at which they arrived) until 8 o'clock the following morning (when they left) not a sound was heard, nor did either the candles or the fire burn blue. The policeman has been in the house ever since, and not the slightest noise has been heard.

It does certainly appear exceedingly strange that these "mysterious" and by some called "supernatural noises" should have ceased from the time of the family leaving the house. If it were a trick, of which there can now be but little doubt, it was an exceedingly clever, although a very mischievous and wanton one. It appears to be a second edition of the Cock Lane Ghost.'

Hampshire Advertiser, 3 July 1841.

'The Globe – learned in matters of natural history – contains the following scientific reason for the mysterious knocking at Clewer ... "'In the West Indies', says Mr Gardiner, the giant cockroach is a noted reveller when the family are asleep. He makes a noise like the smart rapping of the knuckles on a table, three or four sometimes answering each other. On this account he is called the drummer, and they often beat up such a row that none but good sleepers can rest for them.'" After this explanation there can be no doubt that the ghost is only a West Indian cockroach. The dryness of the soil, and the freedom from humidity of the air of Clewer – to say nothing of the genial weather we have lately had – are quite sufficient motives for assigning the noise to a tropical insect. There are many "noted revellers" to be met with occasionally at Windsor, but we had thought that their duties confined them to the castle.'

This last reference to 'revellers' is presumably to those attending royal balls at the castle. There again, given Windsor's uncanny climatic resemblance to Barbardos in this summer of 1841, it is surprising that the Notting Hill carnival didn't set up there. One recurrent feature of 'rational explanations' for poltergeist cases is that they often get more improbable than the poltergeist itself (compare ten year old Marcia Goodin, who in Connecticut 1974 was accused by Police Superintendent Joseph Walsh of lifting up a refrigerator on her own). Notice, for example, that despite these supposedly nocturnal cockroaches, rapping is frequently heard at the cottage in the day, and sometimes never at night. Needless to say, no one ever found any cockroaches.

The Morning Post, 13 July 1841.

'There has been a great deal said, and no inconsiderable excitement created, relative to the mysterious knocking which has been heard at a lonely cottage at Clewer, in the neighbourhood of Windsor. The family, which consisted of an elderly gentleman, his wife and two daughters, and a maidservant, have been induced to leave in consequence. Since their departure, which is nearly three weeks ago, "not a mystic sound has been heard."'

If you take poltergeists seriously, then you can quickly begin to guess that the servant girl was indeed the agent, and that her removal naturally brought the noises to an end. And even if you don't… well, if ever the hoax-test applied it was surely here. I'd be very interested to see anyone stage this as a hoax, using the technology of 1841, with those kinds of witnesses on watch.

5. Poltergeist - or Nightmare?

The Morning Post, 17 June 1851.

'Much gossip has been occasioned at Weston super Mare by a ghost story. John Clark, a gardener, living in a small house near the infant school, declares that his family, and two labouring men lodging at his house, were all in bed Sunday last when, between 11 and 12 o'clock, strange noises were heard below by all of them, resembling the rattling of chairs and tables. The noise having subsided, the inmates of the house, with the exception of Clark, went to sleep. Clarke states that he was wide awake, and heard footsteps coming up the stairs, and presently a man entered the room, and coming up to the bed-side, placed his hands on Clark's face, drew down his arms, and grasped him very tight by his two hands; he held him in this situation for a short period, when the hands of the nocturnal visitor appeared to get gradually smaller, til they became as small as a young child's, when his hold relaxed, and the apparition disappeared. Clark says it appeared to be a man about five feet six inches in height, with very black curly hair and rather stout; that when he was holding him he placed his face very near his, and that he felt his breath very hot, as were also his hands. Clark says he tried to speak and move, but had no power to do either, but immediately his visitor left he jumped up and gave an alarm. He was terribly frightened, and could not close his eyes. He got up, and went to his work on Monday morning, but such was the effect of the shock he received he became very ill, and was obliged to leave his work and go to bed.

On Thursday he told this tale to a man named Tripp, who lived in the same house previous to Clark's occupying it, and from Tripp he received the cheering assurance that he must expect frequent visits from this unwelcome guest, as during the three years he had lived in the house he had appeared to him upwards of a dozen times nearly in a similar way, his last visit being about six weeks before he left the house; the other persons in the house could always hear the chairs and tables rattling downstairs on those occasions, but the visitor never made his appearance to anyone but himself. The men both say the doors and windows were all found secure in the morning, and the furniture in the same position as when left the previous evening.'

In some ways this tale is as richly intriguing as it is baffling. The noises make it sound like a poltergeist incident, and the apparition to imply a haunted house (rather than just the haunted person of the poltergeist agent, who is so often followed from place to place by the uncanny events). But two things complicate the picture. Whilst many poltergeist cases seem genuinely ghostly, ghostly apparitions do not usually have this kind of power over people. They can buffet them and throw them about, but it is very rare to hear of an actual figure holding someone down in this way. The second complication is that Clark seems in many ways to be describing a Sleep Paralysis nightmare – a very real medical phenomenon in which the sleeper is in a kind of limbo state between sleep and waking. When a Nightmare figure intrudes they can be intensely menacing, and can be perceived by the sufferer to be directly causing the paralysis. Yet whilst that would explain some elements of this nightmare, Tripp's warning about his past experiences leaves us wondering. Was it just an unlucky coincidence that an SP nightmare occurred during a poltergeist haunting? Or can ghosts actually *use* nightmares for their own shadowy purposes?

6. The Blackley Boggart.
Blackburn Standard, 10 November 1852.

The peaceable and well disposed inhabitants of the pleasant village of Blackley have been thrown into a state of considerable excitement by the alleged re-appearance of a ghost, or boggart. The house where this unearthly visitor has chosen to take up its winter's residence is a very old building, adjoining the White Lion public house, occupied by a person named William Whitehead, a clogger, who has resided there for the last ten months. He states that he first heard the "boggart" about six weeks ago, when it made noises like the cackling of a hen or the moaning whistle on a railway; and when any of the family stood upon a certain flag in the back room, it screamed like a child. Whitehead removed the flag, and after digging a hole several feet deep, found a cream jug, filled with lime and bones.

A village conference was assembled, and several declared that the bones were those of a human being, and that, at some period, a person had been murdered, and, of course, buried in a cream jug. The "boggart" is heard every night in the week, and occasionally during the day. The ancients of the place declare it is "Old Shaw's wife", a woman formerly resident in the Old Hall, which stood near to the haunted building; others say its appearance is consequent upon the wickedness of some of the neighbours. On Saturday evening, it made greater noise than usual, and on Sunday Whitehead was digging nearly all day in search of the supposed spirit; the cellar steps were removed, and a very large hole nearly sixteen feet long, four feet wide, and above five feet deep, was excavated, of course without success. We advise him next to set a trap; he may catch something.

The family state that a few days ago the kettle (full of boiling water) was removed from the fire to the middle of the house floor. An astrologer from Manchester, with his magic books and glasses has visited the house, and parties looked through the latter to see if they could learn from whence came the spirit. An old man named George Horrix, who once resided in the dwelling, declares that on two occasions he saw the ghost in the shape of a young woman, and it occasionally made noises like the rumbling of stones. Several others give similar accounts, and they do not hesitate to say the house has been haunted for the last 85 years. The man who resides in the building shows no symptoms of fear, on the contrary, he declares he will find out what the annoyance proceeds from before he gives in; but it is vain to tell many of the old people that it is anything but a boggart or ghost, and many families have left on that account. It is rather astonishing to see so many people in the nineteenth century running to visit an haunted dwelling, but numbers are attracted to the place, and the publicans and beersellers will no doubt reap a rich harvest from the boggart hunters. The police officer, who resides only a few yards distant and is professionally a sceptic in all matters relating to supernatural appearances, seems likely to have his duties increased by this troublesome spirit.'

7. The Claverham Ghost

Bristol Mercury, 21 January 1865.

'The good people of Yatton have ... discovered that a mysterious agency is at work in their parish, and high and low, clergy and laity, have as yet been unable to explain the matter. On the road leading from Yatton to Cleeve, and not far from Hollow Mead, is a detached cottage, inhabited by a family named Beacham, and it appears that a few nights ago one of the children, a little boy, was heard by his parents, making a noise as if driving away a cat or dog. He complained that something was scratching at the bedclothes, and a search was made for the intruder, but its whereabouts was not apparent. On the following night the scratching was continued, and now a loud rapping succeeded that was plainly heard by all in the house. Puzzled as to the reason of the noises, the Beachams mentioned the subject to the neighbours, and they having visited the premises, heard the noises likewise, and, after a rigid investigation acknowledged themselves unable to solve the mystery ... [news] soon spread through the whole of the village, and crowds flocked together to listen to the raps, which became louder and louder.

Nor was the excitement confined to the humbler class, for the vicar of the parish, the Rev H.J. Barnard, and Mr Hurd, amongst others, proceeded to the spot, and having listened to the rappings and scratchings, confessed themselves in the dark as to the reason for the disturbance. On Sunday, to crown the ghostly noises, shrieks and wild laughter were audible, while the raps continued unabated. One peculiarity in this matter is that the sounds are more frequently heard in the morning than at night, and before breakfast-time the cottage is filled with startled villagers, who listen to them with breathless astonishment. It is almost needless to add that the dwelling has been well searched, and there being no other house near, the difficulty of accounting for the manifestations is increased. Sometimes there will be heard a sharp series of raps resembling the clapping of hands, and then the sounds will seem to be like violent blows struck with a stout stick, and the scratching prevails constantly. ...

The boy with whom the matter commenced is regarded with mingled feelings of awe, pity and dread, as in some measure the cause of the uproar, and sure enough where he is, although narrowly watched, it would be quite idle to exclaim, "Cease dat knocking". Old ghost stories almost forgotten are now once more rife in Yatton and its vicinity ... The rural population for many miles round have suddenly become decided converts to spirit-rapping, and would, doubtless, consider the Davenport tricks as evidence of supernatural agency.'

As readers may know, the Davenport brothers – Ira and William – were American stage magicians who falsely claimed their effects to be produced by supernatural forces. The comparison is not a good one, given that the Davenports *were* notoriously exposed as frauds, whilst the Claverham Ghost never was.

There may, however, have been a bit of creativity or chinese-whispering between the events and the press reports here. In the hundreds of poltergeist cases I have read, shrieks and laughs, for example, are very rare. Mr Hurd, moreover, would later write to the paper to deny having been there. But the noises do seem to have been very well witnessed; and we should imagine that the Reverend Barnard was pretty trustworthy. One other little detail gives this the ring of truth: the sounds were 'more frequently heard in the morning than at night'. Although this may clash with the stereotypes of ghost stories and films, it matches many other poltergeist cases. In the 1960s, for example, celebrated poltergeist agent Matthew Manning noticed that a lot of events happened 'in the middle of the morning, or early in the evening'. This timing is far from identical with Claverham; but it is interesting that people in cases so far apart *bother* to notice the timing – presumably, just because it is so regular. This may be because the energy the ghost/poltergeist draws on is connected with the natural circadian rhythms of the agent's body. As mentioned, very few poltergeist events occur when an agent is asleep.

The case goes on…

Bristol Mercury, 23 December 1865.

'The Return of the Claverham Ghost.

As our readers will remember, there was a great sensation in Yatton and its neighbourhood some eight or nine months ago in consequence of it being bruited about that there was a house in the occupation of a labourer, in the name of Beacham, haunted by a ghost, every night and morning a most mysterious knocking and scratching being heard upstairs. Hundreds of people visited Beacham for the purpose of hearing this wonderful ghost, but all at once his ghostship disappeared, to the great disappointment of many who felt very anxious to get some clue to the mystery. Nothing, however, has been seen or heard of it til within the last fortnight, when all at once the ghost paid Mr Beacham another visit, and now the report goes that it is distinctly heard between seven and eight almost every night, and Mr Beacham is once more visited by a large number of the inhabitants, who are more alarmed at the visit of the ghost now than before.'

After this tantalising reprise, the ghost falls silent. The recurrence, however, does look plausible. Note, again, the distinct timing – here it is a little different, yet still quite precise, with a regular evening showtime of 7pm. What are we to make of the eleven month gap between the two outbreaks? This kind of interval between poltergeist outbreaks was seen not long ago, in a famous case at Pontefract, Yorkshire (one of the eye-witnesses to which, incidentally, was Geoff Lofthouse, the local MP). The first bout of activity at the home of the Pritchard family in 1966 seemed to use the then fifteen year old son, Philip, as an agent; and the second to centre on the daughter, Diane, aged fourteen. Victorian families being the size they were, there must have been a good chance of two different agents in the Claverham case also.

8. Uncanny Noises.

Hampshire Telegraph, 25 July 1868.

'The haunted house at Muchelney [in Somerset] is one of those extraordinary cases which puzzle the scientific, furnish food to the superstitious, and excite the sneers of the supercilious and would-be knowing. The farmhouse, an old substantial one, stands alone at the entrance to the village of Mucheleny, about three miles from Langport. Its only occupants are Mr Traves, his housekeeper, and a young servant girl. Soon after Christmas last a slight shock of an earthquake, as supposed, was felt in the neighbourhood, and since then the farmhouse has been the scene, from time to time, of the noises and "manifestations" before described in these columns. The most common form is noises resembling at first the running of fingers over a hollow partition, or as if passing rapidly upstairs, and always ending abruptly with a kind of discharge as loud as that of a rifle, but with no reverberation whatever – merely a dead thud – often followed successively, kept up at intervals for days together, and then becoming silent for weeks. For some time the tin cover of a copper in the kitchen was wont to be thrown violently off upon the floor, and the bells about the house to be set ringing. But these are at present quiet, and the newest manifestation is in one of the passages, where a clock stands, with a table near, against the wall, and over it some bridle bits hung upon nails.

About a fortnight since, during Mr Traves's absence in the hay field, the housekeeper and servants were terribly alarmed by the table being turned violently upside down, and the bits thrown off the nails on which they were hung. The females immediately summoned Mr Traves, who came in, and expressing his determination to judge for himself, took a seat near the table and watched. He had not been seated five minutes ere the table was again suddenly dragged, as it were, along the floor, and dashed down. We plainly saw the breakage which resulted, and heard the story from Mr Traves's own mouth. It was only one of several stories of an equally startling nature. The mysterious part is that the walls are entirely unshaken and the floors undisturbed.'

Bristol Mercury, 8 August 1868.
'The "Haunted House" at Muchelney'.

' ... The unanimous testimony is, that, whatever the cause, there are no grounds whatever for the suspicion of trickery and collusion. Mr Traves himself, we would stake our reputation, is too respectable and too honourable a man, to be party to any trickery. The two ladies, his relatives, are totally above anything of the kind. The servant, an intelligent-looking girl, is often not in the house when the mysterious noises are heard and the furniture is knocked about. Moreover, these things happen in broad daylight – rarely by night – and often in the presence of several people who could not fail to detect collusion, and whose testimony is in all cases exactly similar ...

In our article of July 21st, we described the phenomena most generally manifested – the knockings upon the walls, the hammerings as if upon floors or tables, the flinging off the cover of the furnace, the violent overturning of tables, and so forth ... [an eyewitness from a few days ago states]: "We had not left the kitchen long when we heard, from the same direction, a noise as of a heavy table being dragged over a stone floor. Again we ran into the kitchen and found that one end of the deal table ... had been moved about a foot from the wall. The housekeeper was in the act of stepping out of the back door, and, on seeing us running into the kitchen, she said, 'Oh! it is nothing this time. I believe I must have dragged the table with my dress, for it moved as I passed the corner.' The servant, who was at the other end of the kitchen, declared, however, that her mistress was mistaken. She was certain, she said, that her dress *did* not touch the table, as she was looking in that direction when the lady walked towards the door. She asserted, moreover,

43

and in this statement she was supported by the other inmates of the house, that the table had several times before moved away from the wall in the same manner. Not feeling quite satisfied, we requested Mrs Hawker to pass the table again, dragging her dress against the corner as roughly as she could. This she did repeatedly, but found it impossible to move the table, which contained two heavy drawers, without actually lifting it up with her hand, or pressing her side firmly against it.

... The strangest part of the evening's business, however, was yet to come. We were standing at the front door, chatting about what we had seen (all the inmates of the house, except the servant, being either with us or in the larger sitting room) when we heard a great noise in the kitchen, as of something heavy being thrown violently upon the ground. Within three seconds the whole of our party were at the kitchen back door, looking in amazement upon the table to which we have before referred. It was lying across the doorway upside down, with its legs sticking bolt upright in the air. We were fairly on the spot when the servant, who had been in the barton [farmyard], and had, she said, heard the noise while there, made her appearance at the opposite side of the court, running towards the door ..."

...

The writer just referred to ... goes on to say: "The knockings vary as much in loudness as in locality. At one time they are like a regular, gentle knocking, travelling round and round the room. At another time, they can be compared only to the beating of the floors with mallets or to a volley of musketry. On some occasions the noises have been terrific. The people of the village have heard them as they sat in their own homes, and have turned out and surrounded the house, listening to the unearthly row for hours together. The number of excited persons who have thus assembled has sometimes been so great that the presence of the police has been rendered necessary. One day Mr Traves cleared the house and locked the doors, stationing a policeman at the back and watching the front himself. To use Mr Traves's own words, fifty men with mallets could not have caused the awful row which was heard while the house was thus watched, for the loudest knockings appeared to proceed from every part of the house simultaneously."

We have been told the same thing by fifty people. A strange feature in the affair is the character of the noises. They produce no reverberation, as actual hammering would, and do not visibly shake the walls in the least – not so much as to fracture the plaster, although sometimes minute scales of whitewash are picked up about the floors. Mr Traves one day tried the experiment of firing a gun at the doorway, and the report reverberated through every room and passage, producing a totally different effect from that of the mysterious noises, which would appear to be the *echoes* of some primary percussions.

... on Tuesday evening ... a new phenomenon was observed in the dining room ... Miss Hawker, while sitting in the dining room, suddenly felt herself pushed, as it were, out of her chair. She jumped up, and the chair fell completely over. She had felt this once before, some weeks ago, but felt that it might have been caused by some movement of her own ... [now] in a few seconds one of the empty armchairs suddenly performed a similar somersault. The servant was then in the kitchen.'

Two things about this poltergeist case are especially interesting. One is that the agent seems to have been the housekeeper, not the young servant. We do not know the housekeeper's age. She must have been older than the servant, but perhaps in this case not that much. At any rate, the fact that the events often happened in the servant's absence seems to pin that part of the blame on her senior mistress. Second, we have the particular quality of these noises. If they are as loud as claimed, they must have been impossible to hoax. But what is most striking is their peculiar deadness or flatness – the lack of the obvious echo which was heard when Traves tried his experiment with the shotgun. This appears to correpond to the relatively recent scientific findings of physicist Barrie Colvin. Having recorded a number of poltergeist rappings from different cases, Colvin analysed their acoustic signatures. This is a property of any given sound, and in part involves the way the sound builds up, peaks, and dies away. Colvin found, remarkably, that poltergeist noises have their own unique acoustic signature. This cannot be reproduced by ordinary means. Impressively, Traves seems to have noticed this quality, decades before the invention of sound recording or use of acoustic signatures.

9. An Uncertain Case.
Western Mail, 3 July 1889.

'At Marylebone Police Court on Tuesday Sarah Withers, 21, a Welshwoman, was brought up on remand charged with stealing two cambric pocket handkerchiefs, a silk handkerchief, and the pawnticket of a watch, belonging to her master, Mr W.J. Gomersall, a schoolmaster, residing at King Henry's Road, South Hampstead. Detective Sergeant Fox said he had been prosecuting inquiries with Detective Barrett about the prisoner, and they had succeeded in unravelling a very extraordinary history. The prisoner's name was Emma Tranter, and she had been personating a young woman named Sarah Withers. She had been at a number of places where very mysterious things had happened, causing great excitement in the locality. In 1887 she was in service at Shepherd's Bush, where windows were broken by someone – nobody knew who – some property was missed, and prisoner was dismissed on suspicion. Last August she was in a situation at Hackney where there was a great stir in the neighbourhood owing to the mysterious smashing of windows. Two respectable persons living close by were proceeded against at the police court, and were convicted as the guilty persons. At Highgate, where the prisoner was in service, further commotion prevailed owing to the mysterious disappearance of articles from the drawing room table and other articles dropping from the table on to the floor in the most unaccountable manner.

Prisoner had been traced to several other places, at all of which highly suspicious occurrences happened. She went afterwards to one situation where she heard Sarah Withers, a servant girl, applying for a situation and give the lady her name, address, and history. When the prisoner went after Mr Gomersall's situation she used that information. Her home was in Mostyn Road, Abergavenny, from which place he had received information to the effect that the prisoner was charged at the petty sessions there, in January 1887, with stealing some property, and was fined £3. He had ascertained this independently of the prisoner, who had refused to give information. After what had been discovered about the prisoner, the persons who were convicted at Hackney for window breaking, of which they said they were innocent, had now petitioned the Home Secretary on the subject. Mr De Rutzen, in committing the prisoner for trial, said the evidence was certainly of a very extraordinary character.'

Lloyd's Weekly Newspaper, 7 July 1889.

Here we learn that Gomersall's exact address was 39, King Henry's Road; and furthermore, that

'... the prisoner had been in the prosecutor's employment for about three months. Towards the end of May the windows in the house began to be broken, and much damage was done, but the person who caused it could not be detected. The police were communicated with, and detectives were sent to watch the house. They did so for three weeks, but without any result, although the windows still continued to be broken. The conclusion eventually arrived at was that, as the prosecutor kept a school, his neighbours had some ill-feeling against him, and one of them was actually accused of causing the damage. Unexpectedly one day Detective Sergeant Fox went to King Henry's Road, and the prosecutor's door was answered by the prisoner. Mr Gomersall was called to speak to Fox in the front hall, and while they were talking a stone came through one of the windows on the landing on the staircase. Sergeant Fox immediately ran to the basement staircase, and there found the prisoner halfway up the stairs. He called out sharply, "What have you in your pocket? Come turn out those stones!" and a stone at once fell from her pocket to the ground. She was accused of being at the bottom of the mysterious smashing of glass which had gone on for so long, and she practically admitted it. On her boxes being searched the handkerchiefs were found, and she was given in to custody.'

As my title indicates, this one is perhaps too close to call. Some of it looks like genuine poltergeist activity. Moreover, in addition to the articles falling off tables, the long-running window smashing with all those watching police is hard to explain naturally. It looks very likely that Emma was a bit of a bad lot, and it is not impossible that besides theft she was capable of smashing windows, as the officer claimed. But the phrase 'practically admitted it' is rather ambiguous. Did she admit it or not? There are several well-documented poltergeist cases in which young women have been plainly bullied into admitting things they never did, and this may be one. There is one other detail which, for poltergeist experts, is rather intriguing. That is the moment when the stone 'at once fell from her pocket'. Notice that the account does not say: 'she turned out her pocket and a stone at once fell from' it… One of the strangest features of many poltergeist cases is the appearance of objects *from nowhere* (these often being termed 'apports'). If this was a genuine poltergeist case, and thus partly beyond Emma's control, the sudden appearance of the stone could indeed have been an example of this bizarre but widely reported phenomenon.

10. A Voice from Nowhere
Daily Mail, 29 June 1896.

'The Ghost Pleased with Himself.
From our own correspondent. Paris, June 28.
The latest sensation in France is being caused by a ghost. This ghost is haunting a house at Valence-en-Brie, near Montereau, a few miles from Paris.
I visited the house of M. Lebégue, where the ghost "walks", and had the pleasure of seeing some of the effects of its visit. It not only amuses itself by throwing about furniture and breaking glasses, but talks, and even condescends to interfere with the cooking.

On arriving at the house I was taken upstairs to speak with Mme Lebégue, who is an invalid, and whose nerves have not been improved by the late ghostly visitations. "I do not believe in ghosts or spirits", she said, "but some enemy is making my life for the last fortnight a martyrdom."

I walked over the house and observed the stones, and even had the good fortune to hear the voice saying in a sepulchral tone, "I have worked well; I am pleased with myself."

"How do you account for the stones and missiles arriving in the house, madame?"

"I cannot account for it at all. You see," – pointing to the road, "the shutters are closed, and to arrive at the garden one has to pass by the dining room and turn a little to the right."

What is one to infer? Magistrates and gendarmes have searched and watched the house. The conversation of the country is of nothing but spirits, and when I visited the doctor ... at the hospital of the Charité, and explained to him the phenomena that have been taking place, he expressed a wish to visit the scene, and said he would then pass an opinion. The occurrences might be taking place on account of a strong medium being located in the house.

Dr Berillon, whom I also visited and explained the facts, seemed more inclined to treat the affair as a practical joke, and the voice as that of a ventriloquist. I shall return again shortly in company with the scientific men who are going to investigate the phenomena.'

The Star, 2 July 1896.

'If the reports published in the Paris press are to be credited, a house at Valence-en-Brie, near Montereau, is the scene of curious phenomena, or of the exploits of a very clever practical joker. It appears that the supposed ghosts, instead of making their presence felt at night, do so in broad daylight. It is said generally about six o'clock. Though they upset furniture, open locked doors, shatter windows, and generally behave in a most boisterous fashion, what creates the greatest astonishment is the voice which shouts out all sorts of frivolous remarks, mingled with abuse and insults. This voice has been heard not only by the inmates of the house, the family Lebégue, and by the little servant Isabelle Pelletier, but also by some gendarmes, who were summoned to discover the ghost or practical joker. When they arrived the voice, according to the declaration of the Police Commissary ... greeted them by shouting, "Ah, you had better get out of here, you with your dirty boots."

The Police Commissary is, however, very far from believing in any supernatural manifestation, and all the more so because no voice was heard while he and his policemen occupied the house during a whole evening and a night. Mme Lebégue, who is an invalid, is, of course, much disturbed by all the noise, but the persons who hear it most often are her daughter Charlotte and the young servant. The *Éclair* reporter was told that the other day Mme Lebégue, in her bed, said that she was thirsty, and that immediately the voice shouted, "Charlotte, Charlotte, your mother wants something to drink." The little girl, it seems, is not in any way alarmed at the voice, which she hears constantly. As for the servant, the *Éclair* reporter says she seems to be on almost friendly terms with the voice, and that the only thing that annoys her is that she has to put the furniture in order after it has been all thrown about by some invisible agency. The person who is the most persecuted by the voice is young Lebégue, a lad of fifteen. It is said that when the voice was questioned by him it replied, "I am Prince Visky. I belong to a high Russian family", and whenever anyone inquires where he is, the voice invariably replies, "I am at Marseilles." To the objection that in that case he is not at Valence-en-Brie, the answer comes, "Oh, that is no matter. I can be at Marseilles and here too."

Dr Paté, who attends Mme Lebégue, has heard the voice, and is one of those who seem to be the most impressed by its unaccountable character. In relating his experience to the *Éclair* reporter, he said: "I have heard the voice myself, and that several times, like everybody else here. It uses most violent and insulting expressions. Every time I heard it I advanced towards the corner, the wall, or the spot whence the voice seemed to issue, but I could never discover anything, although I made minute searches, to find a crack, a hole, or opening, through which it might have reached my ears. You will admit that is strange. And how can you explain the furniture upset in hermetically closed rooms? And please note the fact that, of the panes of glass that have been shattered, all were not exposed to stones thrown from outside. Some of them are in a passage which could not be reached from out of doors. I must confess there is something in the affair, but what it is I cannot imagine."

M. Delorme, a neighbour, has also frequently heard the voice. Though he cannot discover who it is, he is inclined to believe it must be the trick of a ventriloquist.'

Although poltergeist voices are fairly rare, the documented cases (Macon in 1612; Saragossa in 1934; Enfield in 1977-78) are impressively well-witnessed and reported. And in both Macon and Enfield the tendency to be frivolous or abusive is also found. In Macon, for example, when one of the Protestants of the household piously rebuked the demonic voice, the latter responded: 'you are very holy and very serious in this company, [but] you were not so when you were singing such a baudy song in such a tavern' – after which, 'the Demon sung the whole song before the company', forcing the good Christian to admit this lapse of his younger and looser days. Meanwhile, the Enfield voice can be heard to this day on tape singing 'Row, row, row the boat, gently down the stream'. The singing is bad enough to make a music-lover want to summon a priest, but for all that none of this (including the dirty boots) is exactly the stuff of *The Exorcist*.

55

Indeed, whilst very few real-life poltergeists are demonic or outrightly sinister, they also fail to reveal the great secrets of the universe or the afterlife in any impressively grave manner. Hilary Mantel, in her ghost story *Beyond Black*, may well have got it right when she claims that they are just as likely to twitter on about how you cannot get decent gherkins anymore, as to unveil the ultimate mysteries of either Good or Evil.

Freeman's Journal, 3 July 1896.

'For the past fortnight all Paris has been excited over the mystery of a haunted house at the rustic village of Valence-en-Brie, near the forest of Fontainebleau. The house in question was occupied by a Monsieur Lebégue and his family, and the ghostly manifestation took the form of a disembodied voice, which spoke to everyone who entered the house and uttered threats of all kinds against its inmates. Naturally this was an unpleasant accompaniment to existence in a country house, and M. Lebégue appealed to the psychical experts of Paris in the hope that the "vox et preterea nihil" ['voice and nothing more'] would be made to stand and unfold itself. His house was quickly invaded by journalists in search of "copy", medical men, hypnotists, and curiosity seekers. The ghost kept his head, or – we beg his pardon – his voice in the midst of the excitement. He addressed all comers in the most *fin de siècle* of Parisian argot.

This is the account the correspondent of the *Gaulois* gives of the origin of the mysterious utterances: "On Wednesday 10 June, Isabelle, the young servant, goes down into the cellar to fetch some chips to light a fire. Her candle goes out, and while she continues filling her apron with the chips she hears a violent blow struck close beside her. At the same time, she perceives in the dim light a red rag fluttering in the air, as if carried by a mysterious invisible hand. She is frightened, and wants to run away, but she is, so to say, petrified with terror by an awful roar.

On the following days a voice is heard, at first very weak, but gaining strength little by little till it resembles the hoarse voice of the giant of the fair. Every day the voice ascends. It is heard at the cellar door, then in the kitchen, and soon in the hall and in the rooms of the house. It posts itself at the bedside of the invalid Mme Lebégue, insults Dr Paté, and jeers at the gendarmes who come to inspect the premises. That voice is heard everywhere. It issues from the ground, from the chimney, from under the dishes on the dining table; it accompanies M. Lebégue's son in to his bedroom, and M. Lebégue's little daughter follows it from the first storey down to the bottom of the cellar, where it seems to be stifled in a heap of wood."

The writer of this vouches that he heard the voice distinctly on several occasions, and is himself convinced "that we are in presence of real and impressive manifestations of these unknown forces of man" in which devotees of psychical science so fervently believe.

…

M. Lebégue's son, being evidently nothing of a mystic, loaded his gun, and fired at some words – it is hard to express oneself accurately in the matter – which he heard issuing from the corner of his bedroom. There was, we are told, a cry as of someone in pain, and the "voice" said in a somewhat jocular tone, "I mean to be off now!" He was as good as his word, if we may use the expression. Valence-en-Brie is now without its "voice", and the journalists and doctors have returned to Paris to spin theories out of the mystery. Outside of Stockton's stories we have never heard anything like it.'

This was neither the first nor the last time a gun was pulled on a poltergeist – a number of police officers have done so within living memory (to say nothing of those who simply fled ignominiously from the haunted house in question). Notice, too, the way that the voice gains strength 'little by little till it resembles the hoarse voice of the giant of the fair'. On one hand this is typical of the often gradual build-up of poltergeist noises per se, from (say) rustlings or scratchings to explosive hammering. On the other, the hoarseness of the voice partly foreshadows the famous Enfield case, in which the bass and gravelly tones of an old man seemed to issue from in or near the body of Janet Hodgson.

The American author Frank Richard Stockton (1834-1902) wrote children's fairy stories which were popular in the later part of the century.

Apologies for the apparently rather messy chronology here; but it's not easy to get all the details across in best sequence otherwise.

The Standard, 2 July 1896.

M. Henri Desormeaux, *Gaulois* reporter from Paris: "On Monday, 22nd June, at 7pm, all the panes of the hall window are broken one after the other, not with missiles from without, but from within, as shown by the shattered glass being outside. On Thursday, 25 June, during a thunderstorm, all the furniture in the drawing room on the ground floor is upset. On the first floor, in young Lebégue's bedroom, a looking glass is pierced as by a bullet. It is at that moment the voice says, in presence of M. Daniel D'Aigre, of the *Journal*, 'Well! I have done a good job. I am pleased with myself.' The next morning I am in the hall with two visitors, the servant is in the garden speaking to another person, when I hear at the cellar door the mysterious roar like the monstrous amplification of a sigh of regret."

... Desormeaux appears to think that the intentional or unintentional cause of all these manifestations, is the young servant, Isabelle Pelletier. In other houses in which she previously served, at Sens and at Valence, things were upset without any cause, while she was present or not far off. To explain his hypothesis, M. Desormeaux invoked the researches of M. De Rochas and of Dr Baradue, who think they have discovered the existence in man of a fluid enveloping him, which fluid, in its normal condition is impalpable and invisible, but which under certain conditions is exteriorised and materialised, and rendered capable of impregnating inert objects to the extent of imparting to them a sort of life. In that case the objects become, so to say, a prolongation of the person's body, and when he moves, they follow him ... M. Desormeaux argues that it is possible that the contact with any object pregnant with contrary electricity may determine a return current occasioning the displacement of objects ...

In a letter dated yesterday and addressed to the editor of the *Journal*, Abbé Schnebelin declares he has put an end to the mysterious manifestations ... [He believed that] the author of the manifestations was a human being, who bore ill-will to the Lebégue family. Who he is the Abbé does not say, but he declares that on the urgent request of M. Lebégue, he commenced on Monday to break the occult forces operating at Valence-en-Brie from a distance. He says that at ten o'clock in the evening he had so far succeeded that the voice said, "Good night; I am going away for ever."'

If ever there was evidence not merely for the existence of ghosts, but ghosts with consciousness and personality, this would seem to be it. Given what is said of poltergeist disturbances at Isabelle's other places of employment, she seems the most likely agent in this case. It is interesting, though, that Charlotte Lebégue, the young daughter, hears the voice a great deal too, as her age fits that of a typical agent. No less interesting is the fact that neither girl is frightened of the voice.

Notice, too, the possible causal link between the thunderstorm and the associated tumbling of furniture: it is quite likely that the storm supplies energy for these events, or acts as a trigger on the body of Isabelle. What of the scientific theories of Rochas and Baradue? Although the notion of this invisible 'fluid' now looks slightly quaint, the idea of a field of force around the agent's body is in itself plausible. This was explored by the veteran parapsychologist William Roll (d. 2012), who argued that poltergeist events notably decrease in proportion to their distance from the body of the agent.

Did the Abbé Schnebelin actually have any causative influence on the ghost's departure? It is certainly possible that he had some influence on the poltergeist agent. Given how religious all the household probably was, his actions may have had a psychosomatic effect on Isabelle, and therefore deprived the ghost of the human energy it required.

Ghosts

Anyone who has been paying attention in preceding pages will have begun to realise that it's by no means easy to cleanly separate 'poltergeists' from 'ghosts'. Having said that, part of the rationale of this second chapter is to explore people's fervent *belief* in ghosts during the nineteenth century. The number of cases of false alarm in this area is impressive: at times it seems that, after dark, almost anything could pass for a ghost in the fevered imaginations of the general public in this era. And yet, whilst some such false alarms now look outrightly comical, some are outrightly tragic. Time and again men and women, children and adults, actually died of their fear of ghosts.

Anyone who feels that there are not enough real ghosts in this chapter can be consoled by the very convincing and memorable incidents in Sheffield and Hampstead, as well as by the ghostly apparitions we will meet later on. They can also, perhaps, be consoled by an interesting confession from the author. I have never seen a ghost. But I know a surprising number of people who have. And yet, it took me quite a while to take these stories seriously. Some months into my research on poltergeists, I was thoroughly convinced that these surreal, impossible, uncanny events *did really happen*. Yet I was very unwilling to try and fit ghosts into the theoretical picture I was building up. Poltergeist agents, it seemed to me, were the central key to these supposed hauntings. For a time, then, I tended to stop listening when people brought up ghosts. I have since changed my mind. There are far too many ghost stories, told by so many different kinds of people, to easily write them off as mere imagination. And if you say to yourself: well, no one's ever told me, that may well be because you've never asked. So, yes: ghosts exist, but it does take time to convince yourself of this. Keep an open mind, and if you're still curious at the close of this book, do try Matthew Manning's extraordinary true ghost story, *The Strangers*.

11. The Hammersmith Ghost.
The Times, 6 January 1804.

Come early January a supposed ghost had been terrorising nocturnal wanderers in Hammersmith for around six weeks. On 3 January, one Francis Smith took the law into his own hands...

'The Christmas tricks of this goblin have terminated in two melancholy accidents ... For several nights past, some very silly and thoughtless person had been in the habit of walking about the more lonely vicinities of Hammersmith, attired in a white sheet to frighten women and children; and so far succeeded in acquiring the character of a *dreadful ghost*, as to frighten several poor women almost out of their senses. One woman, the wife of a locksmith, has lost her life through the fright, and now lies dead at Brook Green, and two others lie dangerously ill from the same cause. Much alarm and irritation had of course been excited by these circumstances; and Mr Smith having spent part of his evening at the White Hart public-house, left it, perfectly sober, with a purpose of passing the remainder at a private party, to which he had been invited; but by some means or other, his purpose was changed, and he returned to the White Hart, where, amongst other topics, a conversation about the Ghost took place ... and the great terror and alarm it had excited in the neighbourhood; when Smith went for his fowling-piece, which he brought back to the White Hart public-house, loaded it there with powder and shot, said he would act this night, go and try to meet the Ghost, and certainly shoot it.

It was past 11 o'clock; he preconcerted with a watchman at the place to go up one lane, while he, Mr Smith, should go round by another, the reputed haunt of the Ghost; and as he came through Cross Lane, at the end of Black Lion Lane, he saw a man dressed in white, whom he challenged, and asked who he was. The person made no answer. The night was very dark. After a minute or two, he challenged him again, and told the person in white, if he did not answer and tell who he was, he would certainly shoot him. The man made no answer, and Mr Smith fired at him, when he immediately fell, and instantly died. Smith observing him fall, ran up to him alarmed; but seeing him with scarcely any signs of life, he immediately ran back to the public house, expressed his alarm and apprehension that he had killed a man, and his determination of immediately surrendering himself to some Magistrate ...

Both parties lived in, and were well-known to, the neighbourhood. The deceased was a journeyman bricklayer [named Milwood], who was returning from the house of his father, to that of his father-in-law, where he lived, at a few yards distance. He was in his working dress, which was a white smock and trousers. His sister, who had opened the door to let him out in his way home, had heard the challenge of Smith to him, and the shot which immediately followed; and shortly afterwards saw him lie dead. The discharge must have been very close to the deceased, as his face and shoulder appeared to be much scorched and blackened by the explosion. The contents of the piece entered in a close body his jaw-bone, where it shattered very much, and lodged in the opposite side at the back of his neck. What renders the circumstance still more melancholy is, that the deceased does not appear to have been the person who assumed the appearance of a ghost.

Mr Smith readily surrendered himself to justice, and at six o'clock yesterday evening was brought in custody of the Bow Street officers, from the White Hart public-house, where he had been since morning, to town, and committed to prison.'

Ironically, on the Saturday before his death, Milwood's ghostly clothes had already frightened two ladies and a gentleman, prompting one of them to cry, "There goes the ghost!", and Milwood to respond, 'using a bad oath, "I am no more a ghost than yourself; do you want a punch o' the head?" (*Morning Post*, 14 January 1804).
And the reporter for *The Times* was certainly right in thinking Milwood wholly innocent of any spectral pranks; for the ghostly fraud turned up a few days later:

The Ipswich Journal, 14 January 1804.

'To the satisfaction of most of the inhabitants of Hammersmith and neighbourhood, the Ghost has been discovered in the person and conduct of a *Son of Crispin*! [St Crispin is the patron saint of cobblers] The much-lamented sacrifice of poor Milwood, the bricklayer, had such a powerful effect, that last Thursday evening an information was lodged before Mr

Hill, the Magistrate, against a housekeeper in the town of Hammersmith, by the name of Graham, a boot and shoemaker, who has a wife and three children, for going out at night wrapped up in a blanket, with a design to *represent a Ghost!* Graham was consequently taken into custody and examined before the said Magistrate, who, doubtful how to act without advice in such a case, has taken bail for Graham's appearance. Graham, when questioned as to the cause of his assuming such a frightful being, said, that he had done it in order to be revenged on the impertinence of his apprentices, who had terrified his children, by telling them stories of ghosts. He expected to check them of this disagreeable bent of mind to the prejudice of his children, by presenting them, as they passed homewards, a figure of a ghost, which, it seems, he managed very successfully.

Had this weak, perhaps wicked frolic, ended here, it is likely that no serious consequences would have ensued. Women and children have nearly lost their senses. One poor woman, in particular, who was far advanced in her pregnancy of a second child, was so much shocked at this supposed Ghost, that she took to her bed and survived only two days. She had been crossing near the churchyard about ten o'clock at night, when she beheld something, as she described, rise from the tomb-stones. The figure was very tall, and very white! she attempted to run, but the ghost soon overtook her, and pressing her in his arms, she fainted, in which situation she remained some hours, till discovered by some neighbours, who kindly took her home, when she took to her bed, from which, alas! she never rose. The Ghost had so much alarmed a waggoner belonging to Mr Russell, driving a team of eight horses, and which had 16 passengers at the time, that the driver took to his heels, and left waggon and horses so precipitately, that the whole were greatly endangered. Neither man, woman nor child, could pass that way for time past; and the report was, that it was the apparition of a man who cut his throat in that neighbourhood above a year ago. Several lay in wait different nights for the Ghost, but there were so many by-lanes, and paths leading to Hammersmith, that he was always sure of being on that which was unguarded, and every night played off his tricks to the terror of the passengers. The various reports about Hammersmith would more than fill a Newspaper, some absolutely affirming that they had seen the eyes of the Ghost appear like a *Glow Worm*; others, that he *breathed fire and smoke*, and others again, that he vanished in a moment, and sunk in the earth in their presence! Notwithstanding the discovery and detection, very few will yet venture out after dark.'

Some of these sightings clearly exceeded the deceptive powers of the humble shoemaker in his blanket. But they are certainly matched – as we will see in the case of *Satan's Tomcats* – by some equally improbable reports of other ghostly horrors. Arguably, they also correspond well with the terror not just of frail women, but of the hardy waggoner who fled, shamefully abandoning his trembling passengers.

There again, listening to the evidence of brewer's assistant Thomas Groom at the Old Bailey on 13 January, one is inclined to wonder if Graham was the only 'pretend ghost' in Hammersmith at this time:

'I was going through the church yard between eight and nine o'clock, with my jacket under my arm, and my hands in my pocket, when some person came from behind a tomb-stone, of which there are four square in the yard, behind me, and caught me fast by the throat with both hands, and held me fast; my fellow-servant, who was going on before, hearing me scuffling, asked what was the matter; then, whatever it was, gave me a twist round, and I saw nothing; I gave a bit of a push out with my fist, and felt something soft, like a great coat'.[1]

From the very start of the ultimately lengthy legal saga which the killing provoked, there were signs that the Supernatural was going to haunt the law, as it did in other curious trials or inquests throughout the century. On Friday 13 January, the Jury at Smith's trial was given every encouragement to treat this as an ordinary murder, without obvious mitigating circumstances. Instead, they returned a verdict of Manslaughter. Urged by the Judges to either acquit Smith, or find him guilty of outright murder, the Jury very briefly reconsidered, before finding Smith 'Guilty of Murder'. Yet even as Smith was being led away in a state of shock, under sentence of death, the Lord Chief Baron was taking steps to report the case to the King, who before the end of the month reprieved the accused, on condition that he suffer a year's imprisonment. And come 21 July, Smith was entirely pardoned by His Majesty, having served barely six months (*Morning Post*, 14 January 1804; *Hampshire Telegraph*, 23 July 1804).

Was there some sense that Smith had been frightened beyond endurance when he fired that fatal shot? Did he, for one wild moment, actually think he was shooting a genuine ghost? We get two hints at this intriguing possibility from surviving records. John Locke, the Hammersmith wine merchant who met Smith immediately after the killing, states at the Old Bailey that the accused had said the figure 'advanced to him, and irritated his fears, or something of that sort'. Counsel asked him, 'That he called twice, and the figure advanced to him, and raised his fears more?' and Locke replied, 'Yes, and which was the case certainly.' But most intriguing of all is the testimony of Milwood's sister, Ann ('a very beautiful young woman', as the *Morning Post* helpfully informs us, and one who would scarcely be inclined to provide mitigating circumstances for her brother's killer). Asked what she heard from the doorway where she had just bade Milwood good night, she stated that she 'heard a voice say, damn you, who are you, and *what are you*, damn you, I will shoot you? and whilst they were speaking, the gun went off, and I saw the flash of fire from the gun'. Perhaps the Jury, suitably impressed by those three words, indeed felt that Smith was suffering no human terror when he fired at the thing before him, on that fatal January night.

12. The St James's Park Ghost.
The Times, 16 January 1804.

'The story of the appearance of an *uncouth figure*, in St James's Park, in the dead of the night, had occasioned much conversation amongst the Guards for some time past; and so generally was the fact believed, that, at a late hour on Saturday night, a clergyman entered the Birdcage Walk, and patrolled it for several hours, in the hope that he might meet the figure, when, he trusted, he should detect some person, who, through wantonness, was endeavouring to alarm the neighbourhood. The whole night, however, passed away, without his being able to make any discovery. Indeed, it would appear, that the result of the trail of *Smith*, arising from the melancholy affair of the

Hammersmith Ghost, had reached the *ears* of the *headless woman* in the park, and that she had, in consequence, bade adieu to her nightly visits in that quarter.

The last time, it is said, that this *phantom* was seen was upwards of a week ago, when it was observed, about one o'clock in the morning, to walk with solemn gait, from the Cockpit door to the Canal; but whether it afterwards vanished in the air, or sank into the water, the informant cannot say. It was not until the other day, that the old women about the Park were able to account for the ghost's appearance, and they now recollect, that, about sixteen years ago, a sergeant murdered his wife in the Park, by cutting off her head, and they therefore attributed the phantom's appearance to that circumstance.

The officers of the Guards did not think it worthwhile to investigate this tale of horror, till they had reason to believe that the story had made some impression on the minds of some of the soldiers. Accordingly, yesterday, at one o'clock, the Adjutant of the Coldstream Regiment, went to the orderly room, at the Horseguards, and sent for George Jones, of the 16th Company, for the purpose of interrogating him respecting the *ghost*, as it was said that he was one of the men who had seen, and had been considerably affected by the sight.'

Jones was questioned by the Westminster Magistrate Sir Richard Ford on this, and encouraged to drop his story. He stuck by it, however, and swore the following on oath:

"'I do solemnly declare, that whilst on guard at the Recruit House, on or about 3rd January, about half past one o'clock in the morning, I perceived the figure of a woman, without a head, rise from the earth, at the distance of about three feet before me. I was so alarmed at the circumstance, that I had not power to speak to it, which was my wish to have done; but I distinctly observed that the figure was dressed in a red striped gown with red spots between each stripe, and that part of the dress and figure appeared to me to be enveloped in a cloud.

In the space of about two seconds, whilst my eyes were fixed on the object, it vanished from my sight. I was perfectly sober and collected at the time, and, being in great trepidation, called to the next sentinel, who met me about halfway, and to whom I communicated the strange sight I had seen.
(signed): George Jones, Of Lieutenant-Colonel Taylor's Company of Coldstream Guards."
Westminster, 15 Jan 1804.
To the declaration of Jones, we have to add another connected with the subject, and which is equally genuine:

"I do hereby declare, that whilst on guard behind the Armoury House (to the best of my recollection about three weeks ago) I heard, at twelve o'clock at night, a tremendous noise, which proceeded from the window of an uninhabited house, near to the spot where I was upon duty. At the same time, I heard a voice cry out, 'Bring me a light! Bring me a light!' The last sentence was uttered in so feeble and so changeable tone of voice, that I concluded some person was ill, and consequently offered them my assistance to procure a light. I could, however, obtain no answer to my proposal, although I repeated it several times, and as often heard the voice use the same terms. I endeavoured to see the person who called out, but in vain. On a sudden the violent noise was renewed, which appeared to me to resemble sashes of windows lifted hastily up and down, but then they were moved in such quick succession, and at different parts of the house nearly at the same time, that it seemed impossible to me that one person could accomplish the whole business. I heard several of the regiment say they have heard similar noises and proceedings, but I have never heard the cause accounted for.
(signed): Richard Donkin, 18th Company of Coldstream Guards."
Whitehall, 15 Jan 1801.
After furnishing the above documents, we shall hardly again be accused of having framed the account in

Friday's paper, from a circumstance which occurred ten years ago.'

Come 18 January the *Morning Post* found it 'lamentable that such gross superstition should in the nineteenth century prevail in the mind even of the most silly or uninformed'; and ten days later the source of the mystery was revealed.

Jackson's Oxford Journal, 28 January 1804.

'The ghost in St James's Park, we understand, originated in an application of the Phantasmagoria, by two unluckly [sic] Westminster Scholars, who having got possession of an empty house on the side of the Birdcage Walk, were able to produce the appearance which so greatly alarmed the sentinels on duty in the immediate vicinity of the spot, and has given such an extraordinary subject to the curiosity of the public.'

The Phantasmagoria was a kind of magic lantern, relatively hi-tech for its day, with one of the most successful versions having been invented in the late eighteenth century by a Belgian physicist, Etienne Gaspard Robert. The moral of this story, perhaps, is that one should not believe a ghost tale just because of its arresting details, even if it is sworn on oath. The way that the 'old women about the park' managed to make the events fit a supposed murder also reminds us how easily a ghost can be given an authentic history by those who are predisposed to find it. It would be nice to think that the Westminster schoolboys were awarded an A+ for their technology project on this one, although a tidy caning seems more likely, given the amount of high-ranking time involved in the affair. One can well imagine that Donkin and Jones were very keen to get the lads' home addresses, and personally congratulate them on their ingenuity.

13. Wise Ghosts.
The Derby Mercury, 8 October 1807.

'On Friday morning a party of soldiers, stationed at the Old Powder Magazine, in Hyde Park, surrounded the tree from which the alarming noise has issued that has excited so much alarm within the last fortnight. After cutting part of the tree down, and probing the cavity of the trunk, which is very large, with their halberts, they discovered an owl's nest, with two well-grown owlets, and the old owl along with them. It thus appears, that it was the noise of this family that gave so much alarm to the young centinels, not acquainted with such sounds. Ever since the rumour of a Ghost in the Park went abroad (for that was the first story) the tree has been daily visited by crowds of people, expecting to see the spirit of some fair *Eglantine* walk out of the hollow trunk. Above one hundred people were upon the spot on Friday.'

14. The Mystery of the Paddington Chapel Vault.
The Times, 8 July 1811.

'For several days a boy, nine years old, the son of a tradesman in ... Paddington, had been missing. Not returning home from school at his usual hour, search was made for him. Last Tuesday morning he was found dead in one of the vaults of St George's chapel, Paddington. The body was standing against the wall of the vault. His bag, with his schoolbooks, was on his shoulder; there were several coffins in the vault. It is conjectured that the boy had been led there by curiosity, to see a funeral, and that having been inadvertently shut in, he died of fright.'

Imagine being the person who first discovered this incredible scene. It looks, now, like the opening to an episode of Sherlock Holmes, or Jonathan Creek. A sealed room, a body standing up, uninjured, and... quite dead. There seems to be no record of an inquest into this death; but the chances of the child having died of anything like an ordinary heart-attack, aged nine, must be very slight indeed. The mystery itself is actually simple enough, once you know something about the wild terror which the supernatural could inspire in many people throughout the century. The boy almost certainly did die of fright (possibly caused by vagal inhibition, which produces death by shock within seconds or minutes). He was neither the first nor the last. What makes his case so remarkable is not just that eerie frozen posture – a kind of human monument to the forces of Terror – but the further outlines of the story which that state suggests. Presumably, he was simply too terrified to *even move...*

Three years later, a girl elsewhere in London met a broadly similar fate.

15. 'Two Ghosts'.
The Liverpool Mercury, 14 January 1814.

'Some weeks ago a niece of Lord G-- , a young lady about 12 or 13 years of age, rushed out her chamber in great alarm, explaining, that she had seen the ghost of a female servant who had lately quitted the family but who was still living in London. In spite of all the expostulations and arguments used to remove this mental delusion, she persisted in declaring, that she invariably saw the same phantom on entering the same chamber, and the terror of its appearance had such an effect upon her nervous system, that it was feared her faculties would become disordered; and it was deemed expedient to consult Sir F—M--*. After several ineffectual attempts to dispel the fantasy by which she was afflicted, he recommended that the servant whose figure was thus presented to her, should be procured, and placed in the room, in the exact attitude described by the young lady, that by this means she might be convinced of her existence, and be satisfied that the fancied vision was only the coinage of her own brain. This was accordingly done, and the young lady was conducted to the chamber, which she had no sooner entered than she uttered a piercing shriek, clasped her hands, and exclaiming, "two ghosts! – two ghosts!" fell on the floor in a convulsive fit which, in a few hours, terminated her existence.'

*The medical historian Keir Waddington kindly informs me that this was almost certainly Sir Francis Milman, physician to the élite of the day, including the Royal Family (surviving newspaper accounts suggest that 'Right Royal Toady' would be a fair description – but that is another story again.)

I have spent many a fruitless hour going through Obituaries of the period, in search of someone who fits this girl's class, approximate age, and manner of death. It is not impossible that her family was reluctant to print one, given the embarassing circumstances in which she died (and embarassing, too, for Francis Milman). What we do know is that people can and have died of terror. At one level, the mechanism of this corresponds to what has been called 'Voodoo Death': the classic example would be a member of a primitive tribe who believes they have been cursed or bewitched by someone with the power to kill them (witch-doctor, witch, etc). They perhaps suffer a fit; may foam at the mouth; typically refuse all food and water; and die in between 12 to 72 hours, having gone into a state of radical despair and physical shutdown. Hence, when one Victorian inquest into such a death found the victim to have died from exhaustion occasioned by a shock to the nervous system, they were surprisingly close to the truth.

Interestingly, it seems that the physiology involved here actually has a useful evolutionary point. When the missionary David Livingstone was seized in the jaws of a lion his body went utterly limp, and he felt no pain. The lion, thinking him dead, dropped him and ran off in search of live prey. Now known as 'tonic immobility', this last-ditch attempt to trick your predator clearly has its uses. The problem is when this imitation of death carries on too long, and turns into the real thing. We will meet a rather creative echo of the Livingstone story below.

An impressive number of people seem to have died of terror in 'civilised Europe'. The 'Two Ghosts' case is interesting because the victim was privileged, not poor. We also have a suspicion that this girl saw a *living servant* as 'the ghost' because she was suffering some kind of guilt or other complex about the servant. Perhaps she had been the cause of her dismissal? Perhaps she was in love with her? And perhaps turning her into a ghost was actually rather cathartic and useful – at least, that was, until Sir Francis Milman blundered in…

16. A Ghost in Love.

Trewman's Exeter Flying Post, 8 September 1817.

'Mrs Waters, a widow lady, who, with her family occupies a cottage at Hampstead, during the last fortnight has been much alarmed by unusual noises in various parts of her premises in the dead hour of the night. At first she was induced to believe these sounds proceeded from thieves, but having missed nothing to confirm her suspicions, this idea was abandoned, and one of a more solemn description found place in her breast; namely, that the disturbance arose from some supernatural agency, a belief which was confirmed by both her servant maids, who affirmed most positively that they had seen things which had the appearance of a human figure clothed in white, flitting through the garden after nightfall. The terror arising from the continuance of these supposed visitations from the other world, which were kept a secret from the neighbourhood, at length induced Mrs Waters to apply to her nephew, who at once suspected the cause, and by agreement was secretly admitted on the premises, in company with a friend, without the knowledge of the servants, on Thursday night; when, taking their station behind some trees in the shrubbery, they patiently waited the midnight hour, being provided with a dark lantern, in the event of artificial light being necessary to unravel the mystery.

Soon after one, a figure, enveloped in white, entered the garden from a door leading into an adjoining field, and approaching directly to the house, rattled several of the shutters and doors. This turned out to be the signal of his arrival, and in a few seconds a female came from the house and joined the aerial visitant, which, without much ceremony, encircled her, not in his shadowy, but sinewy arms. While in this state of bliss, the friends approached with as much silence as possible: but not with sufficient precaution to prevent alarm, and before they could secure the spirit, it had vanished, not into air, but into an adjoining pig-sty, which happened to be untenanted, and was filled with dry straw.

The female vanished with as much celerity into the house, and shut the door, waiting in a state more easily conceived than imagined, the issue of the untoward interruption to her joys. The friends having approached the pig-sty, exhorted the evil spirit to come forth, with every argument of which they were masters, but in vain, till at length one of them very deliberately set fire to the straw, the light and smoke of which produced the desired effect, and to their infinite surprise and amusement, out crept a young gentleman, whose parents resided in the vicinity, and who had adopted this mode of carrying on an intrigue with the housemaid. It is needless to say that the shame of his exposure, as well as the danger which he had incurred, operated as a sufficient caution to prevent the repetition of similar idle and mischievous expedients, by which, on more occasions than one, the lives of our fellow creatures have been sacrificed.'

17. Running for Deer Life.
The Times, 28 November 1821.

'A young man, who is an apprentice to a respectable dyer in Carlisle, and who has hitherto manifested a strength of mind which treated all tales of disembodied spirits and "things unnatural" with ridicule, met with a circumstance last Sunday night which excited in his breast excessive terror. He was walking near the Deanery, and in the direction of the West Walls of the city, about eight o'clock; darkness was his only companion, and the winds that howled fearfully above him the only sounds that were heard, save the echo of his own feet. Suddenly, a being, whose footsteps were imperceptible, and whose dimly-seen form appeared to him like nothing in the "earth beneath, or in the waters under the earth", rushed upon him with a hollow tintinabular sound. With the speed of Mercury, the unfortunate dyer fled, but his strange and apparently unearthly opponent followed him with the rapidity of lightning; up a lane and down Blackfriars Street the youth rushed – still, still the light hoofed being was at his heels. At last, when arrived at the Post Office, finding himself run down, rendered desperate as to his fate, and cheered by the light which the place afforded, he turned manfully round to combat his unknown and wonderful enemy --- when lo! nothing was visible save a beautiful tame fawn, with a bell round its neck, which most familiarly approached him, apparently begging for something to eat.'

18. The Gas-lamp Ghost.

The Leicester Chronicle, 30 May 1835.

'On Thursday night week, a considerable degree of excitement was produced in the neighbourhood of the Southwark Bridge Road, in consequence of a rumour that a ghost had been seen, at an uninhabited house in King Street, in which a tragical event is said to have occurred some years ago. Crowds of people collected opposite the house, in front of which stands a tree, and at some distance off the light from the gas lamp completely illuminates that portion of the building next to the street. At the door of this house stood a form resembling a man of gigantic stature, apparently with an immense club uplifted in his grasp, and there he remained fixed, although stones and missiles were thrown by the mob, none of whom, however, had the courage to approach. On the following night, no sooner had the gas been ignited than the same figure was again seen; and a crowd of between 200 and 300 persons quickly assembled opposite the house, when various were the conjectures expressed on the subject, some declaring it to be their opinion that it was the ghost of a former landlord, for whose misdeeds to the poor he, being an overseer, was doomed to revisit the land of the living; others said that the house was filled with evil spirits, and that the "ghost" at the door was placed there, like another Cerberus, to guard the place, and prevent the intrusion of earthly beings. The people, however, soon began to get impatient, and regular attack was made by the mob, who leathered away at the door, at a respectful distance, however, with brickbats and stones. The object of the attack still kept its position, notwithstanding the fierceness of the assault, when some of the more sober-minded of the spectators, fearing for the safety of the house, sent off to the [police station] to give information of the disturbance.

The superintendent (Mr Murray) immediately proceeded to the spot, and had a view of the figure, which had the appearance above described; he, however, advanced to the door; the figure did not retreat, while the crowd stood looking on, apparently with the utmost anxiety, to witness the rencontre between ghost and superintendent. The latter, on arriving at the door, at once discovered that the object which had excited such crowds, and excited such terror in the minds of the credulous, was nothing but the shadow of the tree in front of the house, produced by the light of the gas lamp. In order to do away with the impression that the house was haunted, and prevent the assemblage of people opposite, the superintendent had the side of the lamp next to the house painted, and the shadow at once vanished'.

19. Unholy Choir.
The Standard, 21 August 1840.

'Last week the neighbourhood of St Finnbarr was greatly disturbed for three nights by noises and groans, as if proceeding from some persons in distress; the sound appeared as if in the cathedral; crowds of persons collected round the place; and on Friday last the authorities of the church deemed it necessary to have the corpse of a lady taken up that was buried in the aisle; but she was perfectly dead as when her friends left her. On searching the church some persons went up to the belfry, and to their utter astonishment, there were two old owls, which occasioned all this disturbance.'

20. A Ghostly Old Jackanapes.

Berrow's Worcester Journal, 8 April 1847.

'On Monday Captain Finch, an old officer, was brought before the magistrates of Teignmouth, in the ridiculous character of a detected ghost. He had foolishly amused himself by parading at night lonely places in the neighbourhood disguised in a skin coat, a skull cap with horns, and a mask, in which costume it pleased the old jackanapes to frighten timid passengers. Twice in his ghostly wanderings he had laid hold of, and alarmed into serious illness a poor servant girl; but by some means his identity was made out, and he was brought before the magistrates, who found him guilty of two acts of assault, and fined him 17s for each'.

21. A Ghost Converts A Sceptic.

The Derby Mercury, 7 March 1855.

'That the popular belief in ghosts is not extinct, even in a large town like Sheffield, is proved by a tragic circumstance of recent occurrence. It was currently reported in Campo Lane, at the latter end of last week, that a ghost, "all in white", had made its appearance in the house of John Favell, who lives in Campo Lane, a little beyond the parish church. The story was genuine thus far, that a young woman named Harriett Ward, who lodged at Favell's house, affirmed in the most solemn manner, that she had seen an apparition in the cellar-kitchen. This assertion was made with such an air of credibility that the other inmates of the house – Favell, and his wife, and the wife's sister – could not altogether disbelieve it, though they had no visual evidence of its truth. Favell had heard strange sounds, however, which he thought might have their origin in supernatural agency.

On Saturday evening they felt so much concerned on account of the ghostly presence that for the sake of greater security a friend of the family, a man named Robert Rollinson, who lodges in Court number 24, South Street, Park, was requested to spend the night at Favell's house. Being neither superstitious nor timid, Rollinson acquiesced. He and the other persons went to bed in due time, and Rollinson reported on the Sunday morning that he had seen nothing extraordinary, but towards morning had heard a strange noise that he could not account for. He returned home for breakfast, having first received an invitation for himself and [his] wife to dine with the Favells. His wife at once accepted the invitation to dinner, and seemed to regard the apparition-story as a pleasant jest. She little knew that within a few hours it would prove her death.

She and her husband kept their appointment at Favell's and remained to spend the rest of the day there. It should be here stated, as a circumstance which may throw some light on this strange affair, that all the parties concerned – except, perhaps, the ghost, of whose creed nothing is known – were members of the community called latter-day saints, whose congregational meetings are held at the hall of science, Rockingham Street. To this place Favell and his family and friends repaired, leaving in their house Mrs Favell's sister, Mrs Rollinson, and Mrs Johnson (the person at whose house in South Street the Rollinsons lodged.)

On the return of the party who had gone to the hall of science they were accompanied by several acquaintances who had heard of the apparition and perhaps felt curious to know more about it. Harriett Ward was eloquent on the subject of the vision, and several of the visitors went into the cellar-kitchen to see the ghostly residence and the precise spot where it had been seen. A number of persons had assembled in front of the house, understanding that the ghost was on view, and anxious to have a peep for nothing; but Mrs Favell, feeling annoyed at seeing so many individuals prying at the kitchen window, requested her sister to fasten a temporary blind against it with two forks. The sister, however, had not courage to perform the task, although several individuals had already gone down into the kitchen, preceded by Harriett Ward with a lighted candle. It was at this moment that Mrs Rollinson's disbelief in ghostly manifestations exhibited itself in full force. "Pooh, pooh!" she exclaimed, rather impatiently, "give me the forks, child!", and immediately she descended into the kitchen to hang up the blind. She had not been there many moments when, looking in the direction of the stairs which she had descended, she became suddenly terror-stricken, and seizing the arm of her friend Mrs Johnson with a convulsive grasp, exclaimed in broken accents, "Oh, Mrs Johnson, I saw something on the steps! Take me away!"

This unexpected incident imparted a reality to the occasion which perhaps few present had expected. Mrs Rollinson, in an agony of terror was conveyed up the steps, and immediately afterwards fainted. After a while, her consciousness returned, but for a brief interval, and she assured her friends, in the most earnest and solemn manner, that she had seen on the stairs a female form, dressed in white apparel, and that it approached and rushed past her. The fact of no one else having seen it made no difference to her. She believed the evidence of her eyesight in that instance as she had been accustomed to do on ordinary occasions, and probably nothing could have shaken her conviction that she had seen a spectre. Again she relapsed into a state of unconsciousness, in which condition she was removed in a cab to her lodgings, and died there about noon on Monday. Her death had certainly been caused by the fright she received on the previous day, up to which time she was in perfect health and spirits; and her friends concur in stating that she was by no means of a timid disposition. A coroner's inquest was held on Tuesday, before the deputy coroner (H.P. Badger, Esq) in consequence of the poor woman's sudden death. The hard-headed matter of fact jury could make nothing of the ghost story, so they returned a verdict of sudden but natural death. We are unable to say that this verdict has had the effect of exterminating the superstitious feelings that the tragic incident of Sunday last, and the rumours which preceded it, have awakened.'

22. 'A Child Frightened to Death'.
Bradford Observer, 26 November 1857.

'On Monday morning a little girl whose parents reside in Harvey's buildings, Strand, was playing with some of her companions, when one of them covered herself with a black cloak and mask, and suddenly starting out, so frightened the child that she fell into violent convulsions, and shortly afterwards expired.'

23. A Ghost at Riseley.
Trewman's Exeter Flying Post, 18 September 1861.

'Our readers will no doubt be surprised at the fact that a real and substantial ghost ... has appeared at the village of Riseley. It seems that a certain householder, whom we will call William, retired to rest one evening last week, feeling sure that all the doors and shutters were duly fastened. He had hardly received the embraces of the god of sleep before he heard some very mysterious sounds in the regions below. His first idea was that some person with mistaken ideas with respect to *meum* and *tuum*, was endeavouring to find an entrance into his premises, so that he might enjoy some of the good things of this life ... But no, the sounds he heard were not those of the midnight marauder; they were scratchings, thumpings and runnings, followed by the sound, as it were, of some smothered groans. Naturally, brave William at last got out of bed, lighted a candle, and came down stairs, as he says, "just as he was" ... He had no sooner got down than the awful sounds ceased; he opened the back door and, notwithstanding the coolness of his attire, boldly went out to see if he could there discover the disturber of his rest; but nothing could he find outside. He returned into the house, and scarcely had he entered the doorway when a large hairy object met him with a thump, thump, thump! Poor William with all his bravery was "rather scared", but plucking up his dormant courage, he boldly assailed the object – ghost or no ghost – and soon had the whole satisfactorily explained. It appeared that ere retiring to rest William had accidentally left a small quantity of milk at the bottom of a narrow-necked jug; this milk puss had discovered in her peregrinations, and, in her eagerness to have a taste thereof, had thrust her head into the jug, but was totally unable to withdraw it again. It was in trying to relieve herself of her impromptu head-dress that puss had made the horrible noises which so alarmed the valiant William. However, William was very glad to have seen the ghost; and, as he once more tucked himself comfortably between the sheets, expressed himself to the effect that "he was glad it was no worse!"'

24. 'Frightened to Death by a Ghost'.
Nottinghamshire Guardian, 29 January 1864.

'On Monday Mr H. Raffles Walthew held an inquest at the White Hart tavern, Kingsland Road, London, touching the death of Priscilla May, aged 19 years, who lost her life by the practical joke of a servant in dressing up as a ghost. Mr R. May, No. 145, Kingsland Road, said that deceased, his daughter, was a dressmaker. She was in perfect health when about four months ago she went to Mr Blyth's house in Hyde Park Gardens. She returned three days afterwards looking seriously affected in health. She could hardly breathe. Her nostrils were greatly distended and were plugged. She said that she had been terribly frightened the night before. As she was going upstairs with the governess and the servant, past the bath-room, something all in white threw the door wide open and appeared from the darkness. She said that she instantly fell back screaming into the arms of the governess. Blood gushed from her nostrils, and she was carried downstairs insensible. A doctor was sent for and the servants remained up with her all night. It appeared that the apparition in white was a servant, who dressed her self in white for a practical joke. Deceased never recovered from the shock. She lost her appetite, and her mind became affected. She gradually sank and died on the 19th instant.

Sophia Sturgeon said that she was a servant in the employ of a gentleman, residing at 30, Upper Hyde Park Gardens, Bayswater. On the night in question witness was preceding Miss Clarke, the governess, and the deceased upstairs when she heard a supernatural scream to imitate "a ghost". Deceased gave a scream – like a laugh – and fell. Witness said that Emma Frisley, the nursery governess, came to the door of the bath-room in her white night dress as a joke. Witness would swear none of the other servants were in the secret. Emma Frisley, nursery governess, said that she made her appearance in white merely to frighten the persons going upstairs. The other servants knew nothing of her intention. She told deceased that she was very sorry that she had so seriously frightened her. The whole affair was a frolic out of her own head.

Mr A. Chatterwood, surgeon, said that he was called in to deceased and found her suffering from loss of blood, nausea, sleeplessness, and want of appetite. Latterly she became affected in mind. She would not look at witness, nor answer when spoken to. He believed she died from an obscure affection of the brain conjoined with hysteria. Her death was decidedly accelerated by the fright. The coroner said that the fact of dressing up as a ghost was very foolish and very dangerous. In several cases it produced idiotcy, and in the present instance it caused death. It was but right to consider, however, that the young woman who caused the mischief did not intend anything seriously, and that she was evidently sincerely sorry for her folly. No doubt this case would act as a warning to young persons and in that way do a public good. The jury returned a verdict of death from obscure disease of the brain and hysteria, accelerated by a fright, and that her said death was caused by misfortune.'

Like that anonymous little girl, Priscilla May was one of many people who died of the terror brought on by what now look like hopelessly crude ghost pranks. It is hard to think of a better measure of our distance from the nineteenth century supernatural world than this – not least because of all the trouble we go to, nowadays, to make ourselves scared. In 1857 a farm servant named John Percival spent three months in prison, charged with manslaughter, after gliding about under a white tablecloth, moaning, as 15-year-old John Mitchell passed by, one Monday evening the previous December. Even after Percival had thrown off the cloth and revealed his homely self, Mitchell went home wild-eyed and trembling with fear. In following days he refused food, vomited, and 'raved in his bed'. By Friday evening he was dead. Percival was acquitted in spring 1857 – partly because the doctor testified to Mitchell's very weak constitution; but partly also because the law, interestingly, could not decide if merely *posing as a ghost* was a criminal offence. Many thanks to Alex Landon for passing on the story of Priscilla May.

25. A Hampstead Exorcism.
The Pall Mall Gazette, 12 January 1889.

This story was related by Miss Frith (aka Jane Ellen Panton). Daughter of the well-known artist William Powell Frith, she wrote for a Canadian paper under the signature "Walter Powell".

'There are two rows of old red brick houses at Hampstead, forming an avenue to the church, which houses, built on ground which once belonged to a monastery, are continually troubled by the most unaccountable noises, in one or two cases the inhabitants declaring that the noises, which they *can* bear, have been further supplemented by the appearance of apparitions, which they *cannot*. Not long ago, one of those [houses] possessing the worst of reputations was taken in all innocence by some people who, till they had been in the place sometime, were left unmolested. But very soon steps pattered up and down stairs in the dead of night; doors, previously locked, unaccountably flew open; often there was a feeling, even in the broad daylight, that one was being watched (said my informant) by invisible eyes, touched by invisible fingers. The maids gave warning continually, the children occasionally were frightened, but as months went on without anything actually being seen, the footsteps and rustlings, growing monotonous, were at last almost unheeded, and the household settled down with the firm determination, annoying enough to the ghost, to ignore its presence altogether, a resolution not always strictly kept.

One afternoon a November or two ago the lady of the house sat by the fire in a small drawing-room, shut off from a larger one by folding-doors, reading fairy tales to her little daughter, and as she read she heard someone walking overhead, in a room from which the ghost always started on its peregrinations. She glanced at the child, who was staring into the flames, absorbed in the history of "The Snow Queen", and who, wisely enough, had no ears for anything else, and continued the story without a pause. Soon on each of the shallow oak stairs sounded the well-known pit-a-pat of high-heeled shoes, till the steps, staying a second at the smaller drawing-room, went on to the larger room, the door of which opened and shut with a bang; but nothing disturbed the little girl.

As her mother read on, someone behind those folding doors was turning the handles softly, pacing up and down the floor, moving chairs and small tables, till at last the reader became so nervous she thought she even should have screamed. Instead of that, however, she made some excuse of resting for a moment, gave the book to her daughter, and taking up a lamp went bravely to the threshold of the other room and looked in. The footsteps ceased suddenly, but, peer as she might into every corner, nothing could she see. Just as she was turning back to the "Snow Queen" and the fire, the child ran towards her. "Why mamma", she said, pointing to a windowseat on which the stream of lamplight fell brightest, "who is that pretty lady?" Since then Mrs S, who is a Catholic, has had that restless ghost laid (this is the nineteenth century, five miles from Charing Cross) and with bell and book the priest and the acolyte have done their best to restore peace to Number – Church Row, the consequence being that after that afternoon, spent in sprinklings and prayer, the pretty lady has altogether ceased her visits'.

26. Death by Rumour.

The Leicester Chronicle, 19 November 1887.

'A laundry girl, named Kate Butler, has been discovered to be the author of a ghost scare at Ditton, near Widnes. Arraying herself in a white sheet on Sunday evening she so terrified a woman named Woodward that she is now confined to bed, suffering from shock to the system.

On Monday night Mr Samuel Brighouse (coroner) held an inquest at the Hesketh Arms House hotel, Churchtown, Southport, on the body of a little girl named Jane Halsall, daughter of a gardener residing in Mill Lane. The father of the deceased said that on Wednesday night last he was returning from his work, about six o'clock, when the deceased met him in Mill Lane. She took hold of his hand and turned back with him, saying at the same time, "Father, there is a ghost at Liverpool, and it is coming toward Southport." Witness, knowing her nervous disposition, replied, "Nothing of the sort"; and deceased then said, "the children say so".

On arriving home she said the same thing to her mother, who replied that "the ghost was dead and buried". About half past seven o'clock deceased went to bed with two other children in the room occupied by witness and his wife. She was taken ill during the night and died on Friday afternoon. She complained of pains in her head, and about six hours before death she said, "the ghost is coming".

Dr Hawksley said he was called in to see the deceased. He found her suffering from congestion of the brain, and treated her accordingly. Having heard the history of the case from the father, he was certain that congestion of the brain was brought on through shock to the system consequent upon fright.

The coroner, addressing the jury, said he was sure they all deeply sympathised with the father in the loss he had sustained under such circumstances ... It was a thing he felt very much himself, but he was afraid they had no power over the person representing this ghost even if they could find him. He (Mr Brighouse) could only say that whoever the person was, he was a mean, cowardly, and despicable fellow, and if he saw the account of the deceased's death in the papers he ought to feel heartily ashamed of his foolish proceedings, which led to so tragic a result. That one man should have power by impersonating the ghost to strike terror into the hearts of timid children was fearful to contemplate, and he hoped sooner or later the man would be caught and, if there was a law affecting such cases, that he would be the recipient of such punishment as would be a warning to him and others who were inclined to indulge in such silly freaks.

The jury returned a verdict to the effect that deceased died of congestion of the brain consequent upon fright.'

Notice here how neatly the girl's terror and death match the typical time-span seen in classical voodoo deaths: she meets her father in a state of shock on Wednesday, and dies on Friday. The coroner's belief that the Court 'had no power' over the ghost hoaxer offers us one more instance, meanwhile, of how the law was often baffled by supernatural beliefs or habits.

27. A Reminiscence of my Oxford Days.
Hampshire Telegraph, 22 December 1894.

'This is the only ghost story that I know. It is a true story, and I have never seen it in print, and never heard it explained away ... Here is the story as I heard it.

It is a Brasenose ghost, and it was seen in the early part of the century, at a time when the Brasenose undergraduates were conspicuous among their fellows for profane iniquity. The most audaciously iniquitous of them had banded themselves together into a club. The name of the society was the Hell Fire Club, and its avowed purpose was the promotion of all manner of wickedness by means of song, and jest, and story. The club met in the rooms of the different members in turn, and a notable feature of its gatherings was that there was no chairman. At the head of the table stood a vacant chair; and the theory was that it was occupied by our ghostly enemy, the invisible Prince of Darkness. The dons knew something about the club, but not enough to warrant their interference with its proceedings. But one night the truth was revealed, suddenly, tragically, and supernaturally, to the Principal. It happened in this way:

The Principal had been dining at the adjacent College of Exeter. The hospitality of the Exeter common room is agreeable, and he had lingered late; but about midnight he started on his homeward way. His route lay down a narrow thoroughfare called Brasenose Lane, which separates Brasenose from Exeter. The ground-floor windows, looking out upon the lane, are barred, so that undergraduates may not issue through them upon prohibited nocturnal rambles. And, as the Principal of Brasenose pursued his path along the lane, a strange thing happened, and a strange sight appeared to him.

The college clock solemnly struck twelve, and while the air was still vibrating with its tones, a sudden flash of lurid light illuminated one of the ground-floor windows. The Principal looked, and an awful vision met his eyes. For first he saw an weird and fearful figure – a figure with horns and hoofs and a girdle of fire – the figure of one whom he recognised as Apollyon, the enemy of man. And then he saw that Apollyon had hold of an undergraduate – an undergraduate whom he knew – and was dragging him violently through the window bars.

Then, suddenly as it had come, the vision passed, and Brasenose Lane was once more in darkness. But the Principal had the vague sense that something horrible had happened, and he hurried on to the college gate and rang the bell.

The porter opened to him, and as he stepped inside he heard the sound of many footsteps streaming down the corridor. He questioned the men, and by degrees they stammered out their story.

There had been ... that very night a meeting of the Hell Fire Club in the rooms, from the window of which the Principal had seen his vision. They had sung their blasphemous songs, and told their ribald stories; then, at the last, an undergraduate – the undergraduate whose face the Principal had recognised – had stood up in their midst to make a special parade of blasphemy, and as he blasphemed ... he had been suddenly struck down dead.

That is the ghost story, and there is a wealth of evidence testifying to its truth. For myself I had it from an old man – a clergyman – who was in residence at the college at the time. He told me of what the man had died; but it is something too horrible to write down here.

"And I remember something else," he added. "I remember how the coffin was laid out before the funeral in the college hall, and all of us undergraduates were assembled there to look at it, and to find a warning for our own lives in the horrible fate that had overtaken our contemporary."'
Anon (Lyric).

The Brasenose Hell Fire Club was an imitation of the more famous Hell Fire Club of Medmenham Abbey. It flourished from 1828 to 1834, and its raison d'etre was the defiance of religion and mortality. Real as the Club may have been, we have to suspect that this particular tale is a little too good to be true. It looks, indeed, rather like something from that great academic ghost-story-writer of the era, M.R. James – not least because the figure of Apollyon, from the book of Revelations, appears in both.

28. A Ghost and its Valet.

Dundee Courier, 26 August 1898.

'For three or four nights last week great excitement prevailed in the Anderson district of Glasgow. An unsettled, eerie feeling came over the inhabitants, for a ghost had taken up its abode in their midst, and when nightfall came was seen disporting itself among the tombstones in the old churchyard in North Street. It was about the middle of the week when the spectre made its debut, and the few frightened ones who saw it quickly spread the news, with the result that on the succeeding nights thousands of people congregated in North Street and the streets near with the object of beholding this vistant from another world.

Their numbers gave courage to the crowd, and the more daring among them sat upon the graveyard wall, and peered curiously through the gloom at the tombstones, from behind which every now and again flitted a nimble white-robed figure. For a moment it would stand stiffly erect, its draped arms raised on high, and then it would vanish suddenly, into the grave apparently of some long-deceased inhabitant of this ancient burgh. This continued for two nights, and on the third – always an ominous number – two fearless constables were detailed off to lay the perturbed spirit to rest.

When darkness fell they slipped into the graveyard from Bishop Street, and concealed themselves behind some bushes. Tightening their belts, they bravely awaited the appearance of the spectre on its nightly rounds. They had not long to wait. All of a sudden the mysterious being bobbed out from some obscure corner and stood before them. Their well-tried nerves were now at full tension, and their hearts went pit-a-pat, but constabulary duty had to be done. Forward they rushed, and at the same time a number of lads who were perched on the wall jumped into the graveyard bent on the same purpose as the police. The officers made two apprehensions, one being the ghost, and the other a lad of eighteen named Alexander M'Watt, who, they allege, has acted as the ghost's valet. The spirit was quickly exorcised, and when the white tablecloth was removed there was revealed the corporeal body of little Bobby Tait, of 84 Main Street, shivering with terror in the constabulary grasp.

At the Western Police Court yesterday the two boys were charged with having on the 19th inst. been riotous and disorderly in their behaviour, and caused a large crowd to assemble, to the annoyance of the lieges [authorities]. The two constables gave their statement as to how they captured the ghost , and said that M'Watt had fixed the sheet round Tait. A young woman, who admitted that she had gone every night to see the ghost perform, stated that she saw M'Watt, sitting on the dyke looking on like the rest of the crowd, and when he leaped over the wall he was caught. He did not appear to have any connection with the ghost at all. The charge against M'Watt was found not proven, but Tait, who is fourteen years old, was convicted. Superintendent Andrew said that no doubt such a pastime afforded excellent fun for boys, but he hoped such a sentence would be passed as would act as a warning to others not to entertain the public in a similar fashion. Bailie Robert Anderson pointed out to the boy that this was a senseless freak, and caused much annoyance to people. It could not be tolerated. On Robert promising, however, not to repeat the performance, he was allowed to go home with his mother.'

Vampires

To any readers who feel there should be more vampires in this chapter, I offer many apologies, and two explanations. First: Britain has never been much of a place for vampires, specialising far more heavily in ghosts, witches and fairies. Second: I am just finishing a long book on the topic, in which you can meet vampires from many times and places, across eleven lurid chapters. By way of a small advance preview, I can add that, although vampires did not exist, the people who believed in them sometimes had good reason to do so. One key point here is that very special kind of Nightmare which we met in the case of Mr Tripp, in Weston Super Mare. I have actually had a few of these myself (spookily, only *after* I started researching the topic...) and they can be pretty unnerving, even to a sober rationalist who understands the medical background. Imagine, then, what it felt like in Greece or Russia or Hungary a hundred or so years back, when your nightmare took the form of someone who'd just died; who seemed to have real weight as they crushed your helpless chest there in bed; and who also seemed to be sucking the life out of you as you lay, paralysed and unable to scream... We have some precise data on these experiences; and we know, accordingly, that these apparent vampire attacks were enough, once again, to frighten people to death. If you don't believe me, read on.

29. No Natural Corpse...
John Bull, 15 June 1844.

'A remarkable instance of superstition and ignorance occurred about a fortnight ago at Clausenburg, in Austria. An old woman having died after several other aged persons, the people conceived that she was a vampire, and to convince them that she was mortal, the authorities and the Clergy, exhumed the body, and exhibited it in an advanced state of decomposition. Even then, however, the ignorant crowd were not satisfied, and it was with great difficulty that they were prevented from running stakes through the body to make sure of her destruction'.

30. The Bride of the Vampire.
The Morning Chronicle, 8 October 1855.

'A German paper relates a curious instance of this popular superstition, which recently occurred at Spalatro in Dalmatia: a young and beautiful girl, the daughter of wealthy peasants, had numerous suitors, and from amongst them she selected one of her own station of life. The betrothal of the young couple was celebrated by a grand feast, given by the girl's father. Towards midnight the girl and her mother retired to their chamber, leaving the father and the guests at table. All at once the two women were heard to shriek dreadfully, and the moment after the mother, pale and haggard, tottered into the room, carrying her daughter senseless in her arms, and crying in a voice of indescribable agony, "A vampire! a vampire! my daughter is dead!" The village doctor happened to be among the guests, and he, seeing that the girl had only fainted, administered to her a cordial, which restored her to consciousness; and he then questioned her. She stated that, as she was undressing, a pale spectre, dressed in a shroud, had glided in by the window, rushed on her, and bitten her in the throat, after which he had disappeared; and she added that she recognised him as one Krysnewsky, a rejected suitor of hers, who had died a fortnight before. The doctor attempted to persuade the girl that she must be labouring under some delusion, but she persisted in her story.

The parents and all the guests unhesitatingly believed that she had really been bitten by a vampire, and they were very angry with the doctor for presuming to say the contrary. The next day, nearly all the men of the village, armed with guns, and all the women, proceeded to the cemetery, uttering dreadful imprecations against the vampire Krysnewsky. The coffin of the deceased was dug up and forced open;

and, being raised on end, twenty guns were fired at the skull of the corpse. The fragments of the skull were then collected, and, in the midst of savage dances and cries, were burned in a huge fire; as was the body itself afterwards. The girl was taken seriously ill, and continued to get worse for a fortnight, when she died. She constantly persisted in saying that she had been bitten in the throat by a vampire, but she would on no account allow the doctor to examine the wound. After her death, however, he took the bandages from her neck, and found a small wound in the throat, which had the appearance of having been made by a harness-maker's awl, which had been poisoned. The doctor then learned that one of the rejected suitors of the girl was a harness-maker of an adjacent village, and he did not doubt that it was he who had stabbed the girl. He gave information to the authorities, but the young man hearing that he was to be arrested fled to the mountains, and committed suicide by plunging into the torrent.'

Like me, you may be thinking that this story is wonderful, but too good to be true: rather like a draft for a tale that Le Fanu never quite got around to writing. But the detail about people being angry with the too-rational doctor rings very true: compare the physician who in Greece begged parents not to bury their merely comatose daughter. This man was powerless in the face of communal beliefs in vampires, and the child was indeed buried alive.

Perhaps the main difficulty with this story is the inconsistency between Krysnewsky gliding in the window in his shroud, and the supposed reality of murder by the hand of the rejected suitor. And yet the girl's initial story may well have been inspired by a typical Sleep Paralysis nightmare – as fantastical and seemingly real as so many others were. If so, it is also possible that the girl's imagination of bites really produced them (psychosomatically) from within her own body. Versions of this weird phenomenon have been recorded several times among recent SP sufferers. We would then have to assume that the poor suitor was innocent (notice that he never confesses) and either died accidentally in flight, or committed suicide in terror of a superstitious attack whose like he had witnessed here before. If so, then ironically the explanation of the rational doctor is wrong, and that of the other villagers indirectly right – not least because the girl probably died of fear, like several SP sufferers before and since.

31. New England Vampires.
Leeds Mercury, 4 November 1872.

Citing Providence Herald, 5 Sept. 'The village of Peacedale was thrown into excitement on Thursday last by the report that two graves had been dug up near

Watson's Corner, on the shore of the Saugatuck River. The family of Mr William Rose, who reside at Saunderstown, near the South Ferry, are subject to consumption, several members of the family having died of the disease, and one member of the family is now quite low with it. At the urgent request of the sick man, the father, assisted by Charles Harrington, of North Kingston, repaired to the burying ground, located one mile north of Peacedale, and after building a fire, first dug up the grave of his son, who had been buried twelve years, for the purpose of taking out his heart and liver, which were to be placed in the fire and consumed, in order to carry out the old superstition that the consumptive dead draw nourishment from the living. But as the body was entirely reduced to ashes, except a few bones, it was shortly covered up, and the body of a daughter, who had been dead seven years, was taken out of the grave beside her brother. This body was found to be nearly wasted away, except the vital parts, the liver and heart, which were in a perfect state of preservation. The coffin was nearly perfect, while the son's coffin was nearly demolished. After the heart and liver had been taken out, they were placed in the fire and consumed, the ashes only being put back in the grave. The fire was then put out, and the two men departed to their respective homes. Only a few spectators were present to witness the horrible scene. It seems that this is not the first time that graves have been dug up where consumption was prevalent in the family, and the vital parts burned in order to save the living. A few years ago the same thing was done in the village of Moorsfield, and also in the town of North Kingston'.

Until a few years back, very few people realised that New England once had its own distinctive species of vampire. This changed after the American folklorist Michael E. Bell published *Food for the Dead*. Here Bell explained how vampire beliefs were used to fight the epic killer disease of consumption in the eighteenth and nineteenth centuries. With perhaps several members of the same large family falling victim to this in a relatively short time, surviving kin would sometimes try to save those who were sick by exhuming one or more of their dead, to check that the body was fully decomposed. If it was not – and that might mean just one partially intact organ – they would not only burn the offending heart or liver, but sometimes give its ashes in water to those who were sick, by way of cure. The logic was strange but simple. This supposedly living heart or body was drawing food or life from members of its surviving family. What is so unusual about this is that, unlike the vampires of Europe, the North American demon was able to attack its victims *from a distance*, without actually leaving its grave.

32. Dead Drunk in Vampire Country.

New York Times, 29 February 1888.

The Pester Lloyd reports from Belgrade what narrowly escaped being a fatal case of shameful supersititon. The police found a few nights ago, lying in the street, the body of a man apparently frozen to death. Efforts to revive him having failed, and his identity having been ascertained, he was handed over to his family for interment. The cemetery was a considerable way distant, and as it was being reached, the driver of the hearse told the priest, who attended for the religious service, that he heard some noise in the coffin. The clergyman and others drawing near also heard the noise, and all ran away lest a vampire should issue from [the coffin] and attack them. The driver, terrified at finding himself alone, turned about and drove the hearse to the nearest police station. By this time a knocking was distinctly audible. The coffin was forced open, and the man was found alive and in a very exhausted state. He complained pathetically of the attempt to bury him despite his remonstrances. He was taken to the hospital, and had nearly recovered. He had been spending the evening with some boon companions, and wandering in a state of intoxication fell and became insensible from the cold. Probably the jolting of the hearse revived him. It is a superstition in

Servia and among many Slav people that when a man dies suddenly his spirit returns as a vampire, and preys on his near relatives and friends.'

33. Undead? or Not Dead?
The Leeds Mercury, 14 March 1890.

'A very lurid light has just been thrown upon the life and superstitions of the Russian peasantry by the perpetration of a gruesome crime in the name of what they take to be Christianity. A rich popular farmer died rather suddenly in the village of Sooroffsky. He had been seen in the enjoyment of excellent health on Thursday, and was found dead in his bed on Friday morning. He was prayed for and duly "waked", after which he was carried to the grave, almost all the inhabitants of the village, inclusive of the priest, following him to the churchyard. Just as the body was being lowered, the lid, which had been fastened rather loosely with wooden nails, began to rise up slowly and detach itself from the coffin, to the indescribable horror of the friends and mourners of the deceased. The dead man was seen in his white shroud stretching his arms upwards and sitting up. At this sight the gravediggers let go the cords, and, along with the bystanders, fled in terror from the spot.

The supposed corpse then arose, scrambled out of the grave, and, shivering from the cold (the mercury was 2 degrees below zero F) made for the village as fast as his feebleness allowed him. But the villagers had barred and bolted themselves in against the "wizard", and no one made answer to the appeals he made, with chattering teeth, to be admitted; and so, blue, breathless, trembling, he ran from hut to hut, like a rat in a burning room, seeking some escape from death. At last fortune seemed to favour him, and he chanced on a hut the inmate of which was an old woman who had not been to the funeral, and, knowing nothing of his resurrection, had left her door unbarred. He opened it and entered, and going up to the stove seemed as if he would get inside it, if he could.

Meanwhile, the peasants gathered together, armed themselves with poles and stakes of aspenwood, the only effectual weapons in a fight with a "wizard", and surrounded the cabin. A few of those whose superstition was modified by faith in the merits of modern improvements also took guns and pistols with them, and the door being opened, the attack of these Christians against this "devil's ally" began. The miserable man, dazed by all that had happened that morning, and suffering from cold and hunger, was soon overpowered, and his neighbours, with many pious ejaculations, transfixed him, though alive and unhurt [until that point] with holy aspen stakes to the ground in the court before the hut.

When things had reached this point the priest, who had recovered somewhat from his terror, came upon the scene, with a half-developed idea that perhaps after all the alleged corpse had been plunged in a lethargic sleep and might recover and live as before. But he found the unfortunate man pinned down to the earth with the aspen pales, with no manner of doubt about his death. The police superintendent (Stonovoy), who lived close by, then arrived, and also saw the murdered man, and made inquiry into the manner of his death. The peasants had gone to their daily work, leaving the body, according to the requirements of the superstition prevailing in Russia, until sundown, when they intended to draw out the stakes and throw the corpse into a bog. Cases of this kind are of not unfrequent occurrence in Russia. The press is taking the matter up, but is not sanguine of attaining perfectly satisfactory results, which cannot possibly be achieved until a fair and impartial trial shall be given to education.'

Staggeringly, the reporter was probably correct in stating that 'cases of this kind are of not unfrequent occurrence in Russia'. For other cases in which the 'undead' were simply not dead, see my forthcoming book, *The Real Vampires*.

34. A Vampire Steals the Show.

The Bristol Mercury and Daily Post, 13 April 1895.

From 1877 the American actress, Mrs Brown Potter, was touring the stages of the world more or less continuously for a full decade. And... 'During Mrs Potter's performance of Lady Macbeth in an Indian city, the house was in almost complete darkness, the only light coming from the candle which she carried in her hand. A hideous vampire bat flew in at the window of the darkened theatre, and, attracted by the candle light, fastened on Mrs Potter's bare arm in the sleep walking scene and sucked her blood until the audience was almost hysterical with excitement. Mrs Potter's eyes were closed, and she was completely absorbed in her part. She went through her speech superbly, and as she retired from the stage the bat flew away. Mrs Potter was quite exhausted, and presently fainted. In her intense preoccupation she had not even felt the bite.'

Fairies

For many people, fairies were not gauzy ethereal creatures with butterfly wings, and they certainly were not synonymous with the pretty blonde-haired little girls now likely to impersonate them in school plays. The real fairies were powerful, sinister and frightening creatures. And one frightening thing about them was this.

For centuries, those whose children were in some way abnormal seriously believed that their own infant had been 'taken by the fairies', with this damaged substitute (literally, 'a changeling') being left in its place. In seeking to make the fairies reverse the switch, relatives or neighbours of the suspect child committed startling acts of violence. These could include beating, starving, near-drowning, immersion in poisonous foxglove essence, trial by heat, or exposure in freezing cold. Unsuprisingly, some proved fatal. Such acts of violence are all too evident in these stories. The case of Bridget Cleary, however, is unusual because she was in her twenties, rather than being a child or infant. The Trevelyan affair, meanwhile, is interesting in many ways – not least because no one seems *quite sure* what it actually means.

35. A Fairy Mob.

The Times, 5 July 1837.

The unfortunate and deluded peasantry of the neighbourhood of Tipperary have been excited not a little within the last week by a humbugging story, got up evidently for a similar purpose to the "Wild Fire" or the "Blessed Turf" of the last year, and which has the effect of collecting thousands and hundreds of thousands together almost at a moment's warning, who can then be led on to any act of desperation their leaders may direct. A man named Keating, from near Newcastle [County Down], was taken ill, died, and was buried some short time ago, but a few nights since he appeared to his brother and father, and told them he had been only taken by the fairies, and that if they were resolute, and would bring plenty of whisky, and some of their neighbours, and have each a black-hafted knife, he would be passing the crossroad at Glendalough, at 12 o'clock precisely, at St John's Eve; that they would first see a little man on a fine gray horse, whom they were to let pass, as well as any others, until they perceived him; he would be mounted on a black horse; they were to get between him and the rest, and to cut off the right ear of his horse, when he would be at once out of the fairies' power, and be let home again to them. Numbers in this town and neighbourhood either believed it or pretended to do so, and went off to the meeting, where we are informed, upwards of 1200 persons assembled.

As may be supposed, no little man or gray horse appeared, and all returned again, but what passed there, or why they were called thus together, is as yet a secret. To carry on the humbug, this ghost or fairy appeared on Saturday night to his father again, and told him all was lost by a fellow going in their company who had murdered three men (whom he named) but that he would be passing Ratcliff's Mill, near the spa, in a few nights again, when they would have another opportunity.'

St John's Eve, 23 June, is important in many cultures with regard to the behaviour of, or the danger from various occult forces, including vampires. The incident of the Blessed Turf was a remarkable one in its own right. Despite reference to 'the last year', the most famous instance of this phenomenon occurred in summer 1832. With the threat of cholera on the horizon, people all across Ireland began hurtling around in great numbers with supposed charms against the disease. One of these was a piece of turf, allegedly blessed by priests, and to be burned outside the door of one's house while prayers were said. Obviously enough, this incident (which also involved the intervention of the Virgin Mary in certain places) can be seen as one more episode amongst the many strange tales of magic in the era. At the same time, it is also an impressive testimony to the power of community, given how impressively fast both messages and charms sped across the country in a short period of time, and with the utmost urgency. People were travelling throughout the night, sometimes running up to ten miles to pass messages and tokens.[2] But as we have seen, to English eyes this kind of alarming mobilisation (note the origin of the cognate word, 'mob') of huge numbers of Irish Catholics could easily look like an excuse for political gatherings or conspiracies – hence the claim, in 1837, that people perhaps 'pretended to believe' the tale of the fairy switch as a convenient cover for illicit political meetings.

36. A Changeling Killed.
The Age, 14 June 1840.

'We have often said, and so have most other Protestants, that the man who could bolt such a monstrous lump of superstition as Popery itself, could swallow anything – nay, if he has been able to take *it* down, with all its legends, fables, and absurdities, it is only wonderful that he can find room for anything more. We find, however, that the thing is possible, and that even in Popish Ireland, such an awful exhibition can take place as that described in the report of the inquest on the body of the unfortunate child, John Mahony, which we have taken from the *Dublin Warder*.

"The facts of the case are simply these: a man of the name of James Mahony, who lives on the demesne of Heywood, the property of Charles Riall, had a son of the age of six or seven, a most delicate child. It appears that the boy had been confined to bed for two years with an affection of the spine, and being a very intellectual child, and accustomed to make the most shrewd remarks about everything he saw and heard passing around him, his parents and the neighbours were led to the conclusion *that he was not the son of his father, but that he was a fairy!* Under this impression, a consultation took place at the House of Mahony; and the result was, that the intruder from the "good people" should be frightened away; and accordingly, on Tuesday night last, *the poor dying child was threatened with a red hot shovel, and a ducking under a pump, if he did not disclose where the real John Mahony was*; and so successful were the actors in their scheme, devised for the expulsion of the fairy, that the feeble child, after being held near the hot shovel, and also having being taken a part of the way to the pump, *told them that he was a fairy, and that he would send back the real John Mahony the next evening, if they gave him that night's lodging!* This occurred on Tuesday night last, and the child was dead the next morning."

Here is the father brought to doubt the identity of his own child – brought to believe that the poor creature before him – his own offspring – is a *fairy* – and actually proceeding to *roast him on a shovel* to extort a confession from him as to the whereabouts of the *real* John Mahony who is supposed to have been spirited away! Old women have been burned for witches in the *olden* time in England – but here is an Irish Papist in the 19th century with *many assistants*, seriously proceeding to roast his own child to ascertain if it was a fairy!'

For all the bewildered, anti-Irish indignation seething off the page here, this incident was far from unique, and many other such cases occurred not in Ireland, but in England. Why? The broadest answer is that, in traditional magical cultures, it was not a good idea to look different, or to act differently. Beyond this general rule, some remarkable particular details about fairy changelings have been unearthed by the scholar Susan Schoon Eberly. Why would a family suspect their child to be a changeling? In many cases, because the mother was delivered of an ordinary, healthy looking baby, which, after a time, started to look and behave very differently. It might cry almost incessantly, fail to grow, have wizened features, and be constantly hungry. Oh – and it would almost always be a boy. Eberly found that several genetic conditions can have these kind of effects, adding that inherited birth defects are indeed far more common among boys than girls.

So: aside from your child now looking like a fairy child (sometimes, even if it was pretty, elfin, and blonde, as with the condition called Williams' Syndrome), you also had the problem of it being abnormally hungry, and crying most of the day and night. We can imagine how this would go down in a small cottage, containing an impoverished family with nine or ten children. Perhaps, then, some changeling murders were more or less deliberate. But we should not underestimate the force of purely magical (as opposed to pragmatic) beliefs.

John Mahony partly fits this profile, but is unusual in being older than the many infant changelings who were abused or killed; and unusual, again, in being *too clever* to be a human boy, whereas so many changelings were in reality children with brain damage. And the peculiarly Irish character of this superstition? There is actually something in this. But we can readily assume that our Victorian journalist would be less happy to know that the superstition was *also* peculiarly English. Why? Because one culprit for changeling malformations was phenylketonuria, or PKU, an 'inherited metabolic disease carried by one person in 70 … When two parents who *carry* the disease produce a child *with* the PKU, the child will appear to be normal at birth.' By around six months, however, the typically light-skinned, light-haired and blue-eyed child would suffer seizures, tremors, hyperactivity and extreme irritability, along with slow growth and mental retardation. It may have a small head, and its 'voice will be characteristically whine-y'. And (adds Eberly), 'most children who develop PKU are of English or Irish ancestry'.[3]

37. Away with the Fairies.
Freeman's Journal, 1 July 1848.

'Some months ago, among a detachment of the 2nd Queen's Royal Regiment of foot, quartered at Lanesborough, was a soldier by name Matthew Lally; during his stay there it is thought he made himself intimately acquainted with the occurrences that had taken place among the small farmers and landholders in a district called the Callows, in the parish of Rathcline, for on his return to headquarters he obtained a furlough, and at once proceeded to the Callows, and entering the house of a snug small farmer, named Lally, declared, to the utter astonishment of the old couple, that he was their son, whom they had buried on a certain day, sixteen years before.

On expressing their incredulity he asked them if their son, whom they supposed dead, had not a mark on him? They said he had, on his breast, on which he opened his clothes and showed them such a mark. Some of the neighbours coming in, he called them by their names, and told them of circumstances attending his mock funeral, and of the exact "offerings" each of them gave for masses to be said for the repose of his soul. But to make assurance doubly sure, he insisted on his grave being searched, his coffin taken out, which, when opened, contained not "the remains of humanity crumbling into dust and ashes", but a log of wood. He then informed them that he was "spirited away" by "the good people" or fairies; that he remained for thirteen years among them, and though married to a high-up lady, was sent on earth for a season, with directions to go into the army and learn the new light infantry exercise ... He related to the assembled multitude the fate of many of their friends and relatives, whom he had met "in the hours of fairy revel".

Satisfied now as to his being their son, he was treated as such by his bewildered parents, and presents from all around were showered upon him; all went on pleasant enough till one morning his new mother asked him to assist his father in the operation of planting cabbages; he willingly assented, declaring he did not know how long he would be allowed to remain; after digging with his father for some time the old man went in for a moment to light his pipe, and on his return the soldier had vanished ... he was nowhere to be seen, none saw him pass. Months rolled on, the fairy man was nearly forgotten, when, to the surprise and delight of all, he again darkened his afflicted parents' door; he then stated that he had gone a long journey over the seas, with his patrons the fairies, and that to his surprise he found himself in Mexico, teaching the soldiers of that kingdom the Light Infantry exercise, the better to resist the Americans then invading them; for "it was told him he should be rich by the fairies". So satisfied were the Mexicans with his instructions that they loaded him with riches; and that now he should return to his regiment, with money to purchase his discharge.

He proceeded to Athlone and told the commanding officer that he was involuntary absent – that he could not depend on his not being called away again – and, tendering the purchase of his discharge, declared the Queen would get four better than him for £20: the rules of the service would not allow this, so he was ordered to be tried by Court Martial ... we have heard that he brought several witnesses from the Callows to prove the truth of the foregoing statement, and to swear they saw him dead and buried, and had paid the "offerings" over him. What the sentence was to be has not transpired; for on the minutes of the trial and the extraordinary tale being submitted to the Secretary at War, he, believing the man to be insane, ordered him ... to be discharged ... He returned to the Callows, assuming the fairy man, foretelling events, and promising cures, thereby extracting money from the credulous infatuated poor'.

38. The Trevelyan Changeling Case.

'Extraordinary Cruelty'.

The Bury and Norwich Post, 19 July 1843.

'A most extraordinary case of cruelty to a child has been made public through the instrumentality of the Rev. C.V. le Grice of Trereife, Penzance. Having heard rumours of the ill-treatment of one of the children of John Trevelyan, Esq., of Penzance, by the orders of the parents, the reverend gentleman wrote to inform him of it, and to request him to do away with the report by a public investigation. To this course Mr Trevelyan consented, and on Monday 10th, the parties all appeared before the Penzance magistrates, when Mr le Grice stated the facts as they had been related to him, and Mr Paynter proceeded, on his part, to call witnesses. It appeared from the evidence of a number of witnesses that the child, who was now only two years and nine months old, and a very pretty blue-eyed light-haired boy, had been frequently made to sit across the stalk of a tree, about the size of a man's hat, that lay on the gorund, for a considerable time together; *because he had been changed by the nurse*!

Ann Brown, who travelled with lace, deposed that she was at Mr Trevelyan's, on Friday week, when the child was brought in from the tree by one of the servants. There was a slight scratch on his thigh, a cut on its lip, and blood on its pinafore. The cook said it had had nothing since morning (it was then three o'clock) and was not to have anything til Master's return. The child was sobbing and trembling. The cook said that during the last summer the child had been tied up by the legs, and cut down when it was black in the face.

Jennifer Jenkins, to whom the cook had spoken of the ill-treatment of the child, deposed that it cried til its voice became as plaintive as the wood dove's.

Edmund Kestle deposed that, about a twelvemonth since, when working at Mr Trevelyan's, he heard a child grieving to itself, and found him in a tree, and he was there for more than two hours, and at length it fell out, from hunger and thirst he believed, and then crawled to the house. It fell about three feet. He had heard Mrs Trevelyan order the child to be put there; and had seen Squire Trevelyan, when the child has been in a carriage, kick it over the slope, the child being brought up again by the servant. At another time he saw the child for some time lying on its face on the gravel walk, being put there by Mrs Trevelyan. Another time he was put behind the grotto in a solitary place whilst his father was at dinner. He (Kestle) asked the servants why the child was left out in the wind and sun without a hat, when the sun must have burnt his head. Had seen his head discoloured by the sun; it was "scrotched", and in a "putrifying state". The cook told him that the tie* of the child's bed was filled with corks from porter bottles.

Francis Dale, gardener, deposed, that he had often heard the child crying, and one day got a ladder and reached the wall where he had seen the child sitting or tied to a tree with its clothes over its knees - it was a cold day in the Christmas. He was about one yard off the ground – and appeared suspended with his body dropped. Heard the child one and half hour before he saw him, and one hour afterwards. He had often gone to another part of the garden because he could not bear to hear the child's cries. He hooted like a wood pigeon. He had cried himself to sleep, waked again, and cried himself to sleep a second time.

The Magistrates retired for ten minutes, and on their return, the Mayor said –
"We are unanimous in opinion that the child has been most cruelly and shamefully treated, but there is not sufficient evidence to connect Mr Trevelyan with the ill-usage, for us to send the case to a higher tribunal. It is clear that the ill-treatment had been committed both under the roof and on the grounds of the child's parent – but more particularly on the grounds – and as the evidence does not connect Mr Trevelyan with it, we must dismiss the case."

The uproar in the Hall, and the tumult outside of the assembled hundreds was very great. Hisses and groans were freely indulged; and, we regret to add, that a number of windows in Mr Trevelyan's dwelling-house were broken and the building otherwise injured.

Mr Trevelyan and the family left Penzance the next morning for the metropolis. The populace followed the carriage through the town, and assailed the inmates with yells and hisses.'

* 'The stuffed case forming a mattress or pillow' (*OED*). Particularly if the tie here refers to the child's mattress, this would seem to be yet one more form of torture – having been horribly abused for much of the day, Walter would then have had great difficulty sleeping.

There are three broad interpretations of this appalling story. One is that the Trevelyan family believed Walter to be a changeling, and were using ritual forms of ill-treatment to make the fairies reverse the switch. The second interpretation, however, fits slightly better with that exact phrase, 'changed by the nurse'. Simon Young believes that this refers to long-standing beliefs about 'the wet nurse who changes a child in her care with her own'. One can well imagine relatively impoverished women wanting their babies to have the kind of privilege their employers might offer – anyone who has read Sarah Waters' novel *Fingersmith* will recall a twist on that desire in her tale of Victorian London. The third possibility – and in some ways the most appalling – is that the family was simply punishing Walter for more or less imaginary faults.

Why? Depressingly, because that was what privileged Victorian families sometimes did.

Which of these explanations is the right one? Despite the valiant detective work of Simon Young we do not have as much evidence as we would like. Young is certainly right to feel that *educated* belief in changelings would be very unusual. The Trevelyans were well-off, if not rich (see the surviving house, for example ('The Orchard', Alverton, Penzance); the carriage; the easy escape to London; and, of course, all the servants). Young also thinks that the ill-treatment was not the sort which people (rich or poor) used against changelings.

Coming to the second possibility, Young shrewdly unearths an additional witness statement, in which the lace-seller, Ann Brown, adds: 'I said it's a pretty child and like a gentleman's child'. As he emphasises, the point here seems to be that this looks like Trevelyan's child, not that of some lower-class wet-nurse; it looks *biologically* or aesthetically genteel.

Then we have the third option, of something like 'routine punishment'. This of course staggers the modern imagination. Simon Young confirms for me that the time Walter was found 'black in the face' he had indeed been hung *upside down*. Needless to say, even one of the incidents detailed above would be enough to generate a Social Services Inquiry in our own times. And in a sense the biggest scandal

135

is surely the response of the magistrates to the abuse (whatever motivated it): the verdict looks shamefully like the upper classes closing ranks, and if there was ever a time when popular rough justice was in order, it was clearly now. The Trevelyans were very lucky to escape with 39 broken windows and some heckling.

I owe that precise tally, again, to Simon Young; and it is only thanks to his thorough response that I can even begin to try and make sense of the strange tangle of cruelty and superstition seen here. Young suspects that the Trevelyan parents, considering Walter *even more naughty* than his siblings, may have remarked facetiously that they thought him to have been 'changed at nurse' (ie, so naughty that he could not be their natural child). One or more of the servants, overhearing this, and taking such tales more literally than their (ahem) betters, then connected such a statement with the appalling cruelty which was habitually inflicted on Walter. If this interpretation is true, then it offers us the oddest set of ironies. That is to say: for purely mundane reasons of their own, Mr and Mrs Trevelyan abused their son so badly that their servants, unable to conceive of such cruelty as 'just punishment', came up with the explanation about a boy 'changed at nurse'. And then, by another series of Chinese Whispers, the press shifted this explanation further into the realm of the supernatural. The only way that they could understand such cruelty was to locate its origins in the realm of fairy belief and magic.

We do not know that much about the adult Walter. But, yes – he survived, and there seems to be no evidence that he was more traumatised or neurotic than his peers. Perhaps his infant trials were considered a suitable preparation for the rigours of public school. At any rate, he became a successful army officer, and fought in the Afghan War. Perhaps most bizarrely of all, he retired back to Penzance, where (as Young rightly wonders), 'goodness knows what his memories were of'.

Readers may find it hard to believe that other privileged Victorian families treated their children in this way. If so, they might want to look into the Autobiography of Augustus Hare. When Hare popped out into the world in Rome in 1834, his aunt Maria decided that she would like to adopt him. The fires of maternal love which young Augustus kindled in his mother's bosom may be judged by her speedy reply to this seemingly unorthodox request: "My dear Maria, how very kind of you! Yes, certainly, the baby shall be sent as soon as it is weaned; and if anyone else would like one, would you kindly recollect that we have others." Augustus presently ended up in the less than tender care of his Uncle Julius and Aunt Esther. As well as starving and beating him, they would leave him in a chilly bedroom with a dog howling throughout the night below the window; and automatically take away from the child anything which seemed to give him pleasure, from books through to best friends.

Having said that, even their behaviour pales beside that of the Trevelyans. Imagine the outcry, now, if this was being done, systematically, to a convicted murderer. But Walter was their own infant son – an utterly helpless child abused with appalling ingenuity by his father and his mother. In the end, then, I am genuinely unsure what to make of this case. Fairy beliefs? Changed at nurse? Or ordinary, sadistic Victorian family life? The choice is yours.

39. The Fairies Down Tools.
Newcastle Weekly Courant, 6 September 1890.

'An Irish servant of mine, a native of Galway, gave me the following relation. Her father was a blacksmith, and for his many acts of benevolence to benighted travellers became a great favourite with the fairies, who paid him many visits. It was customary for the fairies to visit his forge at night, after the family had retired to rest, and here go to work in such right good earnest, as to complete, on all occasions, the work which had been left overnight unfinished. The family were on these occasions awoke from their slumber by the vigorous puffing of bellows, and hammering on anvil, consequent on these industrious habits of the fairies, and it was an invariable rule for the fairies to replace all the tools that they had used during the night. And moreover, if the smithy had been left in confusion the previous evening, the "good people" always arranged it, swept the floor, and restored everything to order before the morning. I never could glean from her any good instances of the labour accomplished in this way, or indeed anything which might aid in the formation of an estimate of the relative skill of the fairies in manual labour; and indeed I must confess that on these subjects I never question too closely – the reader will know why.

On one occasion, one of the family happening to be unwell, the father went back to the smithy at midnight for some medicine that had been left there on the shelf and put the "good people" to flight just as they had begun their industrial orgies. To disturb the fairies is at any time a perilous thing, and so it proved to him – for a fat pig died the following day, little Tyke had the measles too after, and no end of misfortune followed. In addition to this occult revenge, the inmates of the house were kept awake several nights by a noise similar to that which would be produced by peas being pelted at the windows. The statement was made with an earnestness of manner which betrayed a faith without scruple.' – Shirley Hibbert

This story offers us just one example of the fairies' recurrent fondness for doing other people's labour during the night –

from sweeping and dusting, through to threshing mammoth amounts of corn. (Surprisingly, this kind of occult assistance has occasionally been credited to vampires – demons who have been known to mend shoes and plough fields after hours.) It also offers another instance of the fairies' notorious touchiness. Almost any change in routine was enough to disturb, anger or frighten them – so much so, indeed, that at times they look almost autistic. (As I will be arguing in my book on fairies, a few of them actually might have been.)

One final detail here can easily be overlooked; but is in fact the most remarkable of all. After having upset the fairies, the family was kept awake 'by a noise similar to that which would be produced by peas being pelted at the windows'. Surprisingly, this was probably not pure invention, but in fact a minor poltergeist outbreak. Whilst many poltergeist agents seem to have been suffering from mundane psychological trauma, others evidently became agents because of the raw energy of fear vibrating off them. In the case of vampire panics, supposed witch curses, and among those terrified by having offended the fairies, the resultant fear seems to have sparked genuine poltergeist phenomena. (Of which, much more in various forthcoming books.)

40. Bridget Cleary.

'The Burning of a "Witch" Near Clonmel.'
Daily News, 27 March 1895.

'The extraordinary circumstances surrounding the death of the unfortunate young woman named Cleary, at Cloneen, near Clonmel, has aroused popular indignation in the district to a fierce pitch. When the prisoners appeared in the streets last night, under a heavy police escort, they were greeted with yells, hisses, and groans by the crowd which followed them to the Courthouse. ... The prisoners were Michael Cleary, husband of the deceased; Patrick Boland, the dead woman's father; Patrick Kennedy, Michael Kennedy, James Kennedy, William Kennedy, cousins; Mary Kennedy, aunt; John Dunne; William Ahearne, and Dennis Gancy, herb doctor. The husband followed the evidence with intense interest, and at last burst out with, "I can't listen to it any longer" ... 'charge against the prisoners was that they, on March 14th, at Ballyvadler, jointly and severally, and with malice aforethought, feloniously killed and murdered Bridget Cleary. Gancy, the herb doctor, was charged with being an accessory before the fact.

Mrs Johanna Burke, wife of a labourer residing near the Clearys, was the principal Crown witness. She deposed that she went up to see Mrs Cleary, who was ill, and met [William] Simpson and his wife outside. The door of the house was locked. Witness asked for admittance, but Michael Cleary said that they would not open the door. While they remained outside, they heard someone saying, "Take it, you witch". When she got in she saw Dunne and three of the Kennedys holding Mrs Cleary down on the bed by her hands and feet, and her husband was giving her some decoction out of a spoon. They forced her to take it, and Cleary asked her, "Are you Mary Boland, the wife of Michael Cleary, in the name of God?" She answered once or twice, and her father asked the same thing. Michael Cleary, she thought, then threw a certain filthy liquid on his wife. They put the question to her again, and she repeated the words after them. John Dunne said, "Hold her over the fire, and she will answer then." They then placed her in a sitting position over the fire. They repeated the question, and she answered, "I am Bridget Boland, daughter of Pat Boland, in the name of God." She screamed, and they put her back to bed. Witness stated that she went back to Cleary's house the following evening. Witness and deceased's husband and others dressed deceased. She sat with them at the fire, and talked about the fairies. Mrs Cleary said [to Burke], "Your mother used to go with the fairies, and that is why you think I am going with them". Witness asked her, "Did my mother tell you that?" She said she did, adding, "She gave [spent?] two nights with them."

Witness made tea and offered Bridget Cleary a cup of it. Her husband got three bits of bread and jam and said his wife should eat them before she would take a sup. He asked her three times, "Are you Bridget Cleary, my wife, in the name of God?" She answered twice, and ate two pieces of bread and jam. When she did not answer the third time he forced her to eat the third bit of bread, saying, "If you don't take it down, you will go." He flung her on the ground, put his knee on her chest, and one hand on her throat, forced the bit of bread and jam down her throat, saying, "Swallow it down. Is it down?" He suspected it was a fairy, and not his wife. He got a lighted stick and held it near her mouth. Witness and her friends wanted to leave the house, but her husband said he would not open the door till he got his wife back. He told his wife he would burn her if he did not get her to answer her name three times. Her answer did not satisfy him, and he threw the oil lamp over her, and in a few minutes she was in a blaze.

At this point prisoner shouted from the dock, "Excuse me, I cannot listen to this any longer."

Colonel Evanson: "You will get an opportunity to speak."

Witness continued: 'Bridget Cleary was burning all this time. Deceased cried out, and the husband shouted, "Hold your tongue. It is not Bridget I am burning; you will soon see the witch going up the chimney." Witness afterwards saw the corpse brought outside the door in a bag'.

The Times, 29 March 1895.

'The funeral of Bridget Cleary, who was burned to death near Clonmel, Co. Tipperary, in the superstitious belief that she had been carried off by the fairies and an evil spirit put into possession of her body, took place at Cloneen yesterday, and was boycotted by all her relations and neighbours. Not one civilian attended the burial, and the rites of sepulture were performed by four police constables. There was no hearse, and the coffin was borne by a common car from Fethard. The significance of this will be understood when it is remembered that the Irish peasantry regard a funeral not only as an expression of respect for the deceased and of sympathy with the family, but as invested with a certain degree of sanctity. The fact is, however, that the people believe – or, perhaps, with a view to the defence of the prisoners, affect to believe – that the real Bridget Cleary will come back, riding on a white horse sent by the fairies, and that if they can succeed in cutting the reins of the horse, they will secure her. With this object there are persons on the watch on the mountains, one of whom is specially provided with a sharp knife to cut the reins.'

The Times, 30 March 1895.

'It was stated that the scene of this terrible crime was in a mountain district, far from any town, and that the people concerned were peasantry of the humblest class. But this is not correct. The village is only four miles from Fethard, a town of great repute in the olden time, and ten miles from Clonmel. Michael Cleary, the husband of the deceased, was a cooper, who had learned his trade in Clonmel, and his wife was a dressmaker who was apprenticed and spent some time in the same town. They lived happily together in a neat slated cottage, one of the labourers' cottages erected by the Board of Guardians, and well furnished. Michael Boland, father of the deceased, lived with them, and they were in comfortable circumstances for persons in their station in life. A representative of the *Daily Express*, who visited the place has ascertained that on the 5th Mrs Cleary complained of a violent pain in her head, and was subject to fits of shivering, and next day she was unable to leave her bed. A doctor was sent for from Fethard, and pronounced her to be suffering from nervous excitement. She grew much weaker, and some of the neighbours volunteered their opinion of the malady. An old man and his wife came to see her, and announced that the woman in the bed was not Michael

145

Cleary's wife, that one of her legs was longer than the other, and that she was a fairy ... Father Ryan denounced the outrage in the strongest terms at Mass last Sunday in Cloneen Chapel, and called upon those of his hearers who knew anything of the affair to communicate with the authorities.'

The Times, 6 July 1895.

Reporting on the close of the 'trial of Michael Cleary for murder of his wife by burning her as a witch' (Dublin, 5 July), *The Times* records the following sentences:

'Michael Cleary, 20 years penal servitude; Patrick Kennedy, 5 years penal servitude; John Dunne, 3 years penal servitude; William Kennedy, 18 months; Patrick Boland and Michael Kennedy, 6 months each'.

Throughout the century, the law was often stumbling over supernaturally-inspired crimes for which it had no precedent or guidelines. And here, the fairies made legal history. For, though originally charged with wilful murder, Michael Cleary was ultimately convicted of manslaughter, and thus spared the death sentence – all because the Judge recognised the husband's genuine belief in Bridget's possession by the fairies. Notice that the first report here can only begin to make sense of Bridget's death by classing it as a witch-burning. In reality, perhaps the most important link between witch and fairy beliefs was the tendency to single out people who looked or behaved differently: from dwarves through to children with PKU, or adults with mental illness. Bridget was evidently suffering from some kind of mental health problems, and the change in her personality and behaviour was enough to convince her husband that this simply could not be his wife. Improbable as this may seem to us, the same kind of belief existed in Russia. There, the mentally ill could be taken for vampires, and killed accordingly.

Witches

In England, the Witchcraft Act of 1736 outlawed witch prosecutions, drawing a hard line between the legitimised persecutions of the previous century, and the newly-enlightened present and future. By 1736 the last legal execution of a supposed witch was already a distant memory: the victim was Alicia Molland, at Exeter in March 1685. There again, the last 'Guilty' verdict delivered by a jury had been imposed on an alleged witch, Jane Wenham of Walkerne in Hertfordshire, much more recently. In 1712 Walkerne only escaped with her life because the Judge on this case secured a pardon for her after the trial. The split between this educated Judge and the probably less educated jury is telling. In the eighteenth and nineteenth centuries, the privileged élite often shows signs of being effectively 'in denial' about the official witch-hunts of the past. Could their educated ancestors really have *done* this? Although they clearly had, it was not unknown for a Victorian writer to try and claim that the witch-hunts from Elizabeth I through to Charles II were purely popular affairs – a notion which flatters the politically, socially, and intellectually powerless masses to an astonishing degree.

How did this élite feel, then, on the occasions when they were forced to suspect that popular witch beliefs were as widespread, as serious, and as potentially dangerous as ever? The following cases give us some idea. And an abundance of other evidence shows that witch-beliefs in this century were in one basic way very similar to ghost-beliefs. Simply: "if in doubt, suspect a witch". The reasons will usually be mundane (family sickness; milk failure in your cow; pure bad luck), and the victim would – to us at least – often seem disappointingly bland. Anne Burgess, for example, seems to have nothing more sinister about her than a bearing 'of rather imposing gravity'. There again, the impression that being disabled – a dwarf, a deaf-mute – made you a likely witch-suspect is rather more startling to modern eyes. Examples of this also abound in vampire country – and at times the consequences there were still more horrific than the sad death in Sible Hedingham.

The violence which these beliefs provoked is clear enough. What is less obvious on the surface is what this violence sometimes means to those committing it. 'Cutting a witch' was essentially a magical strategy against your supposedly magical enemy. The main point of it was to take the witch's power away. What looks like spontaneous, angry violence is therefore sometimes often much more tactical, controlled and impersonal (see Framwellgate, below, for a very striking example).

The lessons of such tales are numerous. One is the basic failure of Victorian Progress to make headway against beliefs stubbornly ingrained and handed down, orally, for centuries. Another is that, to get rid of such beliefs, you need not only to make people feel more physically secure – you need, also, to give them another system of explanation for their problems. More subtly, there is also a sense that at times personal antipathy mingles with magical belief: this seems to aggravate the attack on Burgess, and perhaps also that on Dummy, the mysterious old Frenchman of Sible Hedingham, Essex. In a few rare cases the 'witch' actually is to blame – either for their evil reputation, or for far more serious crimes. We begin with one of these.

41. 'Witchcraft, Murder, and Credulity'.
The Times, 26 October 1808.

'A plot, accompanied by most unprecedented instances of credulity, was on Monday developed before the Magistrates ... in this town. The parties were Mary Bateman, of Campfield, near this town, and William Perigo and his wife, of Bramley [in Leeds]; she the witch, and they the dupes. It appeared that in August, 1806, an application was made to this woman by Perigo to cure the wife of a complaint which was not stated on the examination, but which we suppose to be what is called among people of her rank "nervous" ... Mary, with becoming *modesty*, declined to undertake the cure herself; but said, that she had a friend at Scarborough, a Miss Blyth, who could "read the suits", and collect from them the knowledge requisite to remove all corporeal and mental maladies, and, as a preliminary, required, that Perigo's wife should send her flannel petticoat to Miss Blyth, in order that she might from that article of dress, collect a knowledge of her disorder. The petticoat was sent, and a propitious answer returned, wherein it was required that the medium, Mary Bateman, through which all communication between the astrologer and the patient was to be made, should have four guinea notes presented to her, and she was in return to give Perigo four other guinea notes, enclosed in a small bag, into which, if either his own curiosity, or the still stronger curiosity of his wife, should induce them to look, the charm would be broken, and sudden death would be the consequence. Strange as it might appear, the wife of Perigo never looked into the enchanted bag to the day of her death. Soon after the four guineas had been given to Mary Bateman, a letter arrived from Scarborough, directing that another guinea should be paid into her hands. Similar requests were repeated and complied with, till forty guineas had been thus extorted from these infatuated people, under a promise, however, that they should, by and by, be allowed to open the bags, and these bags, they were told, would be found to contain all the money they had advanced.

About six months had now expired, and the business of fraud and delusion still went on. Miss Blyth could not, while certain planets ruled, sleep on her own bed, and in order to promote the comfort of the "wise woman", Perigo was to buy her a new bed, with all the necessary appendages, and send it to Mary Bateman, through whose hands it was to be transmitted to Scarborough. The bed, etc, which cost eight pounds, was bought, and notes, to the amount of thirty pounds more, paid at various times into the hands of the impostor. She next demanded a set of china; this was also furnished; but she complained that the tea cannister was not sufficiently handsome to set before the genteel company kept by a lady of her distinction, and demanded a tea caddie in its stead; which demand was also complied with.

Perigo and his wife, thus drained of all the money they had in the world, and all the sums their former good credit had enabled them to raise, and the wife's health still growing worse rather than better, they became impatient to look into the mysterious bags, and extract from them the wealth they contained. Their clamorous impatience probably became troublesome, when, as it should seem, to silence their importunity, Mrs Bateman received, as she said, a packet from Scarborough; this packet contained a powerful charm, which was to be mixed up in a pudding ... and of which Perigo and his wife were to eat, but on no account to allow any person to partake with them. The husband ate sparingly; he did not like the taste; but his ill-fated wife, less scrupulous, ate freely. They both became sick almost immediately, and continued in the most deplorable situation for 24 hours: the wife lost the use of her limbs, and after languishing five days, died on the the 24th of May, 1807, a victim of credulity. Perigo recovered partially; but from that time to the present has never had the perfect use of his limbs. Part of the pudding was, by way of experiment, given to a cat, and it died; some fowls also picked up other parts of it, and shared the same fate. Contrary to the direction of Mary Bateman, Perigo applied to a Surgeon in this town for advice, and was told by him that he had taken poison, but fortunately not in a quantity sufficiently large to occasion his death.

After the death of his wife, it is natural to suppose that the husband would possess sufficient fortitude to emancipate himself from the fangs of this wicked woman: this, however, was not the case; she had thrown her toils over him, and though the wife might not have been, as she supposed, bewitched, it is pretty evident the husband was under some such influence. From May, 1807, til Wednesday last, the charm continued to operate, and the spell could not be dissolved. At one time he went to Manchester by the direction of this Jezebel; at another he sent her one of his wife's gowns; again she contrived to coax or threaten him out of another gown, petticoats, and the family Bible! And last of all she demanded from him a bushel of wheat, with three seven-shilling pieces enclosed. His creditors at length became impatient, and in the hopes of getting any part of his property back failing, he determined to brave all danger and look into the mysterious bags, whose contents he found were not worth one penny.

The bubble now burst; and after having kept the business an entire secret from every soul living, his wife alone excepted, for upwards of two years, he laid his hopeless case before some of his neighbours; by their direction Mary Bateman was apprehended; when brought before the magistrates, she in part confessed her delinquency, and admitted that there was no such person as Miss Blyth in existence, but that the whole was a mere phantom, conjured up to forward her vile purposes. The magistrates have committed the offender to the House of Correction, whether to be tried for swindling or to be removed from there to the County Gaol, to take her trial for wilfull murder, we are not informed.

On searching the house of this woman (who has a husband and several children) the bed and some other articles, the property of William Perigo, amounting in value to about ten or twelve pounds, were found, and will be restored to the owner. It is worthy of observation that Mary Bateman is the person whose hen laid an egg about two years ago, at the bank in this town, bearing this marvellous inscription, "Crist is coming."'

Anyone keeping even a rough tally of the sums paid out in money and goods will have been impressed by how profitable the occupation of magic-worker could be c.1806. Professor George P. Landow of Brown University notes that Victorian 'servants, who had all living expenses taken care of, earned as little as £10/year', whilst 'some poor vicars at mid-century earned as little as £40-50/year'.[4] Given that Bateman managed to extract a silver watch from another victim, James Snowden, and further sums from an aged widow, Judith Cryer (*Leeds Mercury*, 29 October 1808) she may well have been living far more comfortably than her local minister was.

42. Cutting a Witch in Somerset.
The Morning Chronicle, 8 April 1823.

'The most intense curiosity was excited by the name of three females on the calendar, on a charge, under Lord Ellenborough's Act*, of maliciously cutting and stabbing an old woman, a reputed "Witch", with intent to murder her. The Grand Jury, however, after consulting the Learned Judge upon the singular case, threw out the bill on the capital charge of maliciously cutting under Lord Ellenborough's Act, and returned a true bill against the three prisoners for an assault.

Elizabeth Bryant, the mother, aged 50, Elizabeth Bryant, the younger, aged 22, and Jane Bryant, aged 15, the two daughters, were charged with having maliciously assaulted Anne Burgess. Mr Erskine ... stated the case to the jury.

The reputed witch, Anne Burgess, was then called. She is a fine hale-looking old woman, 68 years of age, of rather imposing gravity. She deposed – "I know the prisoners, the mother and the two daughters. They live about a quarter of a mile from me. On the 26th November I went to her house (Mrs Bryant's) and met her in the passage, which is dark. I said, 'Betty Bryant, I be come to ask you a civil question, whether I bewitched your daughter?' [laughter]. She said, 'Yes, you have, you damned old witch; you have bewitched her for the last twelve months'; and she said she was 10l. the worse for it, and she would be totally damned if she would not kill me. They all came out together and fell upon me. The little daughter drew out my arm and held it, whilst one of the others cut at it. The eldest of them said, 'Bring me a knife that we may cut the flesh off the old wretch's arms.' They tore my arms all over with an iron nail."

The old woman here described the manner in which the prisoners performed the operation. She was ill from the wounds on her arm. There was a woman who accompanied witness, came in and dragged her away from their fury. It appeared further that witness and her friend cried out murder as loud as they could, and a mob assembled in the street round the door, but they did not choose to interfere, and it was exclaimed that the old woman, on whom the prisoners were exercising their fury, was a witch. Two of the prisoners, the mother and the elder daughter, continued to hold the old woman as she struggled on the ground for her life (as she expressed it), whilst the younger daughter, with the first instrument that came to her hand, a large nail, lacerated her arm in a dreadful manner. This was done for nearly ten minutes, the mob standing by the whole time, and the old woman was only rescued, as it appeared, by the vigorous efforts of her companion. She did not doubt that if a knife had been in the way when she presented herself at the door, she should have been murdered.

Cross examined – "Do not the people of Wiviliscombe (true or falsely, I don't say) account you to be a witch?"

The old woman (with great agitation) – "Oh dear! Oh dear! That I should live to be three score and eight years old and be accounted a witch at last. Oh dear, what will become of me?"

"Well, it is very hard, certainly, but do they do not account you to be a witch?"

It was some time before the old woman could give an intelligible answer, but she said she had never been accounted a witch in her life (God forbid) by anyone, before the prisoners circulated it about the town that she was, and had exercised her infernal influence over one of them. She always tried to live righteously and peaceably without doing any harm to any one. She was greatly afflicted at the injurious supposition.

The apprentice to Mr North, a surgeon at Wivilscombe, deposed that on the night in question the prosecutrix came to him to dress her arm, which was dreadfully lacerated. There were fifteen or sixteen incisions on it, of about a quarter of an inch deep, and others of an eighth of an inch ... she bled very severely; witness dressed her arm, and as she was very healthy, it got well fast; witness was ill for about a month in consequence of the attack.

...

Mr Erskine said he could adduce evidence, which would show the gross delusion under which the prisoners had laboured; and he was perfectly willing they should have any benefit they might derive from it. ... An old woman, Elizabeth Collard, was then called, who said she was an acquaintance of the older prisoner, and met Mrs Bryant on the morning of the day on which the assault took place, not having seen her before for a long time; witness said we were talking about our troubles, when she told me, that her troubles were greater than mine, or any body's troubles, for they were not mortal troubles; she said her daughter had been bewitched for the last 12 months, and that she had been to consult old Baker, the Devonshire wizard, about her case; she said he had given her a recipe against witchcraft, and that blood must be drawn from the witch to break the charm; she said that old Mrs Burgess was the witch, and that she was going to get blood from her; she was in such a way that I thought she would have gone immediately to Mrs Burgess to have drawn blood, but I advised her not, and to let old Baker punish her if she was really the witch.

Mr Justice Burrough – "Who is old Baker?"

Witness – "Oh! My lord, he is a great conjuror, the people say. He is a good deal looked up to by the people in these parts."

Mr Justice Burrough – "I wish we had the fellow here. Tell him, if he does not leave off his conjuring he will be caught, and charmed in a manner he will not like."

The witness resumed – "I pitied the woman, she was in such a world of troubles; and besides that, she has had a great many afflictions with her family, but she appeared to feel the bewitching of her daughter very deeply. I asked how the witchcraft worked upon her, when she told me, that when her daughter was worked upon, she would dance and sing, just as if she was dancing and singing to a fiddle, in a way that there was no stopping her before she dropped down, when the fiend left her. Whilst the fit was upon her, she would look *wished* (wild or frighted) and point at something, crying, there she stands, there she stands (the witch). I felt for the daughter very much. Her state is very pitiable, my Lord."

Mr Rogers addressed the Jury in behalf of the prisoners. He said, that to attempt to deny that a verdict of guilty must be given against the miserable females at the Bar, would be to insult the understandings of the intelligent gentlemen whom he saw in the box. The observations he was about to make to them, would be rather for the purpose of showing the unfortunate delusion under which the prisoners had been actuated; the infamous fraud that had been practised upon them [presumably by Baker]; their miserable afflictions; and to induce them (the Jury) to give with their verdict a recommendation of mercy to his Lordship.'

There then followed some debate about this between Burrough, the Judge, and Rodgers, as counsel for the defence. Erskine, for the prosecution, stated that he would not try to aggravate the sentence, and that he would be content with any sentence which discouraged such crimes in the future. Burrough hoped that Baker would be prosecuted if guilty as described; and went on to address the prisoners.

' – "Your conduct, Mary Bryant the elder, is of a most aggravated nature. Instead of going to a Magistrate for the redress of any injury which you might have conceived you had suffered, you allowed yourself to be acted upon by an infamous man, and to carry into execution the exploded and horrible notion, that in order to get rid of the affliction of your daughter, it was necessary to draw blood from the supposed witch. There is little doubt that if a weapon had been at the moment within your reach, you would have acted upon your notion to the extent of committing murder upon the poor old woman, for you called out in your rage, 'for a knife to cut the flesh off from the old witch's bones'. As it was, you and every one of you stood in peril of your lives for the offence you had committed, but that I considered it not to have come within the intent of the Act of Parliament. It was my doing that you were prosecuted for this assault, instead of being tried for your lives, but you cannot be allowed to escape without some punishment. You have been guilty of a great, a gross, and very abominable crime, and though, in consequence of the certainty that your mind was at the time labouring under a delusion, I shall act in the most lenient manner towards you, compared with the sentence I should otherwise have passed, yet it is necessary to visit you with punishment that will cause you and every body to remember that it is at the peril of severe punishment, if they act upon such ignorance and folly. The sentence which I feel it my duty to pass upon you is, that you be each further imprisoned in the county gaol for the space of four calendar months."

We have seen (continues the reporter) the paper which the man Baker gave to the poor dupes to wear as a charm against witchcraft, and also the recipe or direction for breaking the charm, of which the following is a copy *verbatim et literatim*:

"The Gar of mixture is to be mixed with half pint of Gen (ie, Gin) and then a table spoon to be taken mornings and at 11 o clock, 4 and 8, and 4 of the pills to be taken every morning fasting, and the paper of powder to be divided in 10 parts, and one part to be taken every night going to bed in a little honey."

"The paper of Arbs (ie, herbs) is to be burnt a small bit at a time, on a few coals, with a little hay and rosemary, and while it is burning read the two 1st verses of the 68th Salm, and say the Lord's Prayer after."

As the preparations were taken by the ignorant creatures, it could not be ascertained what they were, whether medicinal or mere rubbish, as is most probable. But we are positively assured that after the rites had been all performed, such was the effect upon the imagination of the poor girl (aged 22) who fancied herself possessed, that she has not had a fit since. The act of drawing blood from the supposed witch, remained to be performed, in order to break the charm entirely, and to prevent it from returning.'

* Lord Ellenborough's Act of 1803 was actually aimed at preventing abortions – one of the possible means being cutting or stabbing of the pregnant mother. Given that Anne Burgess was 68, the Act looks rather obviously irrelevant for this case. The initial attempt to invoke it may again reflect the confusion which the law often displayed when faced with the various superstitious or magical crimes of the lower orders.

'Old Baker' was just one of many 'cunning-men' and women of the period – often resorted to in cases such as these. Two things are especially memorable about this sad case. One is the sick daughter, crying out eerily that she can see 'the witch' before her: this scene could easily have been plucked straight out of the Salem witch panics of the 1690s. The second, perhaps most remarkable, thing is the Court's insistence that the accused were 'labouring under a delusion' when they attacked Anne Burgess. It is solely because of this educated belief that the sentences handed down are so light. What does this tell us? It implies that, for the educated Judge and lawyers, the only way to deal with the minds of Bryant and co was to assume that they were in some state of *temporary* insanity when they attacked Burgess. Of course, they were not. The attack was the logical outcome of habitual beliefs, which, as Bryant told Collard, had been on her mind for the last 12 months. And if the mob standing by watching the attack dissented from these beliefs, then why did no one lift a finger to help Anne Burgess? This judgement, then, offers us a beautifully contained distillation of a general problem: the gap between You (the educated powers) and Them (the humble masses) was so great that you could never truly begin to get inside their heads.

43. 'Witch-Burning in Dublin'.
The Standard, 3 July 1827.

Sunday 24 June last, 'about four o'clock in the afternoon, an immense crowd of men, women and children (between 300 and 500 persons) were observed rushing down Marlborough Street, near Thomas's Church, shouting and yelling, and tossing up something in the air, which was sometimes caught by one, and sometimes by another, and occasionally fell to the earth, where there was a scramble for it, and it was again tossed from one to the other, amidst the most diabolical yells, which, on a nearer approach, were distinguished to be "A witch! A witch! "Burn the witch!" "Drown the witch!". She proved to be a very decently dressed, dwarfish, deformed female, whom these monsters had suddenly seized upon; and whenever she fell to the earth, during their tossings, fiend-like women rushed upon her, with horrid shrieks, tearing her clothes to pieces; all parties, crying out, "Now we have her!", "Now we have her!" "We'll burn or drown her!", and directing their course to the river. At length a young gentleman, apparently about 18, after appealing to several well-dressed spectators, to aid him in saving the poor woman from being torn to pieces, which they, from terror of the mob, declined doing – rushed into the midst of these hell-hounds, and courageously bore the helpless female under one arm, while with the other he made his way through the crowd, who then directed their vengeance against him; crying out, "The witch's husband!", "The witch's husband!", pulling, pushing, and tripping him, and pelting him with mud, and whatever came to their hands; so that he was bedaubed from head to foot. In making his way down Cumberland Street, and Mecklenburgh Street, he appealed to three or four soldiers who were looking on, and who directly surrounded him, and two gentlemen then aided him, one of them taking one hand, and her rescuer the other of the poor sinking dwarf, and pulling her through the increasing crowd, to the police office in Henry Street (nearly a quarter of a mile) for safety; the new escort came in for their share of mud and abuse. At the Post Office a few policemen luckily came up, and were compelled to do ample justice with their sticks on the savage crowd, before they got the poor creature into the police office: she was not able to speak for some time, from ill usage and terror – and then returned lively thanks to her deliverers; she gave her name, and said she resided with a relative, Mrs --, at No. --, in Camden Street; and observed, that though she had been frequently gazed at, so as to distress her feelings, she had never before met with violence. She was sent home, the back way, after some time, with an escort of police.

The transaction can be borne testimony to by hundreds of persons in the neighbourhood above mentioned, for the disturbance was such, that every window was thrown up as the savages approached. And, this is in the *Capital of Ireland*! and in the nineteenth century.'

44. You Can't Always Trust Your Mother...
Freeman's Journal, 29 July 1842.

'Shocking Case of Superstition.
An instance of gross superstition occurred at Market Rasen last week. A man named Radley, a brick-maker ... has been for the last four years in a low state of health; he attributed his affliction to the agency of witchcraft, and actually accused his own mother, an inoffensive and honest woman residing at Rasen, with practising it. The most absurd and nonsensical

remedies were tried by the deluded man and his family to drive away the "spirit of evil"; horse-shoes were nailed to the door; a bottle was hung reversed over the fire place, having the cork stuck full of pins; and the poor old woman was even cruelly whipped, as she states, by Radley's wife, through the street, but all to no purpose. The man got no better, and at length he determined to try the last, and, as he believed, sure remedy, namely, to "draw blood from the witch". Having met his mother in the street on Wednesday 12th, he accosted her, and offering his hand, asked how she was; surprised at the sudden change in his behaviour (for he had not spoken to her for two years before, though living close by), and suspecting some collusive design, she attempted to pass him without accepting his proffered hand, whereupon he seized hold of her, and inflicted two deep scratches on one of her arms with the point of some sharp instrument which he had concealed in his hand. The wounds bled profusely. This is only one of many cases supposed to be practised in this neighbourhood.'
West Lindsey, Lincolnshire.

45. Veterinary Magic.

Northern Star, 15 Apil 1843.

'At Cornwall Assizes, Bodmin, Fred Peter Hatton, a country looking bumpkin, was indicted under the 9

George II*, for pretending to exercise witchcraft, and thereby obtaining the sum of 3s from one Jenny Francis. The prosecutrix was an old woman who had consulted the conjuror respecting a lost heifer. This case was made out, and the jury, under the direction of the judge, returned a verdict of not guilty. It was then stated, to the evident surprise of the learned Judge (Cresswell) that there was another indictment upon which the prisoner must be tried, and it turned out, indeed, that there were four against him for the same offence.

In the next case also, "the learned Theban" had been consulted by a person who had had cattle die in a suspicious manner, an intelligent and respectable looking farmer who ought to have known better, named Nottle. The directions which the prisoner had given to detect the person suspected of having poisoned them, were: "When you get home, kill the calf (which was one of the cattle ill) and take out his heart. You must stick this heart full of pins, and, writing the name of the person you suspect, pin it to the heart. You must then roast and burn the heart to a cinder, and whilst this operation is going on you must read over the 35th Psalm three times."

On receiving these instructions, Prosecutor asked what he had to pay? The prisoner replied that he usually charged £1 for this job, but that he would charge him only 10s. The money was paid. The prisoner was found guilty upon this indictment, but an arrest of judgement was moved on a technical objection to the form of the indictment. The prisoner had to be tried on a third case, which was postponed.'

* Under the Witchcraft Act of 1736, those pretending to have such powers could be tried for misdemeanour – an interesting legal irony, given the very different trial that such claims might theoretically have catalysed in 1734.

46. Ducking a Wizard.
Essex Standard, 2 September 1863.

Hedingham Special Session, 25 August.
'Emma Smith, a married woman, of Ridgwell, Samuel Stammers, builder, and George Gibson, bricklayer, of Sible Hedingham, were charged with the following extraordinary and cruel assault on an old deaf and dumb Frenchman, whose name is unknown, his sobriquet being "Dummy". Mr Cardinall prosecuted; Mr Jones defended the male prisoners. Mr Cardinall, in his opening address, stated that the prisoner Emma Smith alleged that she was bewitched, and believed that the old man had practised the evil art upon her, and this had led to the assault upon a defenceless old man of seventy.

John Petitt, a shoemaker, of Sible Hedingham, deposed: "On Monday evening, 3 August, I was at the

Swan public house at Sible Hedingham; there were about 20 people in the tap room, among them were the prisoners and old Dummy; Gibson and he danced about the room, and Gibson wanted him to kiss Mrs Smith, but he did not; Mrs Smith said she would give Dummy 3 sovereigns to go home with her; I afterwards saw him outside the house, sitting on the ground; Mrs Smith caught hold of him and dragged him on the ground towards the brook, and I thought both went into the water; I saw the old man in the brook, and Mrs Smith was gone away; he went to the opposite side, but Mrs Smith pushed him back; she did this several times, but at length he got out and sat down on a heap of stones; the woman struck him several times with a stick on the head and shoulders; I told her not to do so, and she then kicked him; there was a crowd of 40 or 50 people standing by; George Jenkinson offered to see the old man home, and Dummy went off down the lane, along which the brook runs; presently I heard a splash, and on going up the lane I saw the old man in the water again. Mrs Smith was by the side of the brook, and the prisoner Stammers was helping the old man out. Gibson was not there. I heard a woman's voice call out, 'Swim him in the mill head.'"

Henrietta Garrod, ten years of age, stated: "I saw Gibson and Dummy dancing in the Swan; they fell down once; he tried to make Dummy kiss Mrs Smith; Mrs Smith slapped Dummy's face; Gibson gave him some beer; about a quarter past eleven o'clock I heard a noise, and went down to the Swan again; I saw Dummy sitting on a stone heap and Mrs Smith shoved him into the brook; I saw Stammers shove him into the water once; Mrs Smith pushed him into the water several times; she asked for his stick, and presently I saw her with it; she struck Dummy on the head twice, and repeatedly across the shoulders; she called him a devil, and said she would serve him out as he had served her out; then somehow he got near the water, and Mrs Smith shoved him in; he tried to call out, 'murder'; Smith took hold of his shoulders, and Stammers took his feet, and they rolled him into the brook; I saw Stammers jump in and get him out; I am sure he put him in first; they got him out and laid him on the grass; Mrs Bruty and others then got him home.'"

George Jenkinson backs this up, adding that there was about a foot and a half of water in the brook; and that no one interfered to help Dummy. He also implies that the attempt at getting Dummy and Smith to kiss was a way of 'making it up' between them. Tellingly, no one really knew how old Dummy actually was: reported estimates of his age vary from seventy, to 76, up to 86. The three sovereigns seem to have been an attempted bribe: either to get Dummy to come to Smith's house and remove the supposed spell, or to lure him there for the purpose of assault.

'W.V. Fowke, Esquire, Guardian of Sible Hedingham (at whose instance the prosecution was instituted), described the old man's condition on the following morning, when he was in a state of collapse, and greatly bruised about the head and shoulders. His clothes, in which he had slept, were wet and muddy, and he screamed when he was undressed. He was removed to the Halstead workhouse on the following day.' Assistant Medical Officer Mr A. Meggett 'stated that he examined the old man on the 5th at the workhouse, and found him suffering from bruises upon the arms, head and shoulders, and from bronchitis recently contracted. He was now confined to his bed, and in very great danger, though not absolutely in dying circumstances.'
Smith was retained in custody and Stammers bailed at £50.

Freeman's Journal, 1 October 1863.

'On Tuesday Emma Smith, aged 36, and Samuel Stammers, 28, were brought before the bench at Castle Hedingham, charged with having caused the death of a poor old Frenchman, who was called Dummy, by putting him into a brook, when already suffering from a severe illness. The female prisoner was the wife of a beershop keeper in the village of Ridgwell, about six miles from Hedingham, and Stammers a master carpenter in a small way of business. The victim of this superstition was deaf and dumb, and his age was supposed to have been about 86 years. Being unable to express himself, and being of a somewhat vivacious disposition, he was accustomed to make use of energetic and somewhat grotesque gestures, which caused him to be regarded with considerable awe. He lived alone in a wretched hut. Who he was, or whence he came, could not be ascertained. For the last seven or eight years he had resided in Sible Hedingham, and previous to that he lived in Braintree. There is little doubt that he gained his living to a great extent by telling fortunes, if not by pretence to witchcraft. Some hundreds of scraps of paper were found by the police in his hut after his death, and upon most of them were written questions which, neither in the style nor their subject matter say much for the enlightenment of the district. In the hovel besides were found between 400 and 500 walking sticks, a quantity of umbrellas, some French books, a number of tin boxes, a bag of foreign coins, chiefly of the French empire, and about a ton of rubbish, which it was impossible to classify in the inventory that was taken. The chairman said that the bench had resolved to send both prisoners for trial at the next assizes.

The prisoner Emma Smith was then formally asked what she had to say. She replied in a peculiar voice that she would tell the truth. The man had come to her house first. He spat upon her, and told her that after a short time, she should be ill, and she was ill. A doctor came to her twice in one night, but could not cure her. The man Dummy came to her shop ten months ago, and asked leave to sleep in her shed. She let him, but in a few days when she wanted him to leave, he made signs, and wrote on a door that she should be ill in ten days. He made her ill and bewitched, and she went everywhere, but no one could set her right again. She was afraid no medicine could do her any good.

The Chairman: "Are you aware of the nature of the charge against you; that you caused the death of the old man by your conduct on 3 August?" The prisoner: "That night I went to the Swan very bad. I went up to the old gentleman, and asked him to go home with me to do me good. He said he would not go. Gibson took him up and put him in my face, and told him to kiss me, but I did not want to do that, as I had a husband of my own. A number of plaiters of straw for bonnets came in, and said, 'how bad this woman is'. They got him out. Some shoved him, some pelted him with mud, and did more to him than I did. I begged and prayed he would go home with me, but he shouted he would not unless he liked. I do not deny that I put my hand to his head, but I was so bad that I could not lift a dog, and this man here (Stammers) took him by the heels and thighs and threw him in the water, and then he (Stammers) jumped in and got him out. I may die any moment, there was only one there who did touch him, and that was Mrs Bruty, who said she was afraid of him. That is the truth." Stammers simply said he was not guilty.' Stammers was bailed, and Emma Smith committed because she could supply no bail.

This report is a tricky one to decode. On one hand, we can well believe that people as superstitious as this were frightened by Dummy's crude sign language. What, though, of the fortune telling, and 'pretence to witchcraft'? The slips of paper do certainly suggest the former. But it is quite possible that, until things turned dangerously sour with Smith's psychosomatic complaint, Dummy was indeed 'regarded with considerable awe' rather than with outright terror. That is: like so many witches of popular culture, male or female, he was considered *powerful*, and could use this power for good or evil.

The Essex Standard, 11 March 1864.

This includes a long report, citing the evidence of many witnesses. Both Mr Pearce for the prosecution, and Mr Philbrick, for Stammers, stated that it was impossible for Dummy to have lived much longer, given the state of his kidneys, as revealed by post-mortem examination.

One witness from the Swan stated that Dummy drank 8-9 pints of beer while there (which would explain why he was sitting down outside.) It also seems evident from Dummy's response to Emma Smith's request (for him to come with her) that he could lip-read. In a grim irony, he allegedly made signs that he would rather have his throat cut.

The sentencing was as follows:

'Judge: "I take into consideration the state of health of the woman, and also the fact that you, Stammers, endeavoured to get him out the moment your attention was drawn to his danger; but I am bound to pass a sentence which I hope will act as an example, which is that you severally be imprisoned with hard labour for six calendar months."

The prisoners were then removed, Mrs Smith being in an almost fainting state.'

47. "May we Burn Your Hair, Please?"

The Bradford Observer, 24 December 1868.

The Newcastle Chronicle states that on Monday night the police officer stationed at Framwellgate Moor (near Durham) was summoned to the house of a Mrs Howe, whose daughter was stated to be in a dying condition, and anxious to tell the officer something before she expired. The officer proceeded to the house, and was told that the girl Howe had been at service with a Mrs Carter at Pity Me, and that while there she had been bewitched by an old woman of some 90 years, named Sarah Judson, who was always tormenting her, and who was about to devour the girl or tear her to pieces. They wished, therefore, to obtain the sanction of the officer to a visit they intended to pay to Mrs Judson, in order to draw her blood, and thus exorcise her. He told the father and mother they must do no such thing, and having told them of the consequences that might follow such a foolish step, he left them. Soon afterwards, however, the family summoned to their aid a "wise man" named Jonan Stoker, and headed by this worthy, they betook themselves to the cottage of the supposed witch, at Pity Me. Stoker asked Mrs Judson, on confronting her, for a portion of her dress to burn, but this demand she indignantly refused to comply with. He then produced a pair of scissors, and, seizing hold of the old woman, snipped off a lump of ribbon from her cap, throwing the piece into the fire. Mrs Howe, at the same moment, seized on Mrs Judson's arm, and soon succeeded in drawing blood. The whole party then made off for their homes at Framwellgate Moor, satisfied that they had overcome the Devil.'

48. Protection Money.
Aberdeen Weekly Journal, 6 September 1888.

'During the past year an old woman living near the town [of Capitalo in Mexico] has been exacting a monthly tax from the fathers of families to prevent her from taking the lives of their children by sucking their breath in some mysterious manner, her pretence being that she was a witch, and had a mysterious power over life and death. She lived in a little hut, in which she kept all the paraphernalia of witchcraft – a cat, a broom, a dead crocodile, etc - and was in the habit of going out on the neighbouring mountains and looking for hours steadily at the horizon, and when in town would mystify the inhabitants by making incomprehensible gestures, writing strange characters in the dust, and otherwise terrifying the simple villagers. Recently a child in one family died suddenly, and as the father had refused to pay the monthly tax to this witch, it was rumoured that she had bewitched the child, an impression which grew stronger and stronger.

Finally the godfather of the child, a man named Medina, met the woman in a street of the village, and said to her, "Why did you kill my godchild?" The witch replied, "Because its father did not pay me my tax." "Well, neither will I pay that infamous tax," he replied. "Then," said the witch, "I will kill your child." "Well, you will not kill it, for I will kill you." He then beat the old woman to death, and his act was sustained by the whole villlage. He has been arrested for murder, and his trial will bring most of the old people of the village to Mexico as witnesses in his behalf. The lawyer for Medina is Emilio Romero'.

This kind of case does seem to have been rare. Many 'witches' were really just unlucky and powerless scapegoats. But not all. Dummy seems to have had some powers in the minds of his Essex neighbours, as did an equally tragic Russian woman, Agrafena Ignatjewa (below). Perhaps most strikingly of all, when two British army officers, St Clair and Brophy, stayed in a small Bulgarian village called Derekuoi in the 1860s, they found that the village witch was arguably the most powerful person there. She was more or less salaried; turned to in all cases of sickness; and even the priest would seek her help over something he had lost. Indeed, this woman did genuinely seem to have had the power of life or death over villagers. If someone believed themselves seriously ill, they would consult her, and she would measure a length of cloth against their arm. If this magic ritual declared that they would die, then they actually did – out of sheer terror, hopelessness, and fatalism, as far as we can tell. We will meet some other striking cases of collusion between witches and priests below.

49. A Witch and a Poltergeist.
Sheffield and Rotherham Independent, 9 October 1889.

'Considerable commotion has been created in the neighbourhood of Salisbury by a case of supposed witchcraft at Homington, about four miles from the city. The person said to have been bewitched was a little girl named Lydia Hewlett (9), and her father is a Primitive Methodist local preacher. Some time since the girl saw a gypsy steal some onions belonging to a neighbour, and subsequently mysterious knockings were heard in the cottage where the girl lived. Some boards of the bedroom where the sounds were heard were pulled up, but the rappings were not explained, and by and by it was noticed that the knockings seemed to follow ... the little girl. These knockings were, it seems, generally heard near the girl, and when no one else was in the room; but it has been alleged that when some one else has been with her the rapping has been heard.

Some one conceived the idea that the child was bewitched, and a number of questions were put to the supposed spirit. According to the replies (given by means of knocks) the gypsy was the cause of all the trouble. She (the gypsy) had dark hair, was 4'8" in height, was married, had seven children, and was 28 years of age ... [28 raps]. The questions were preceded by the words, "in the name of the Lord". Canon Kingsbury heard knocks, and believed that the girl herself did not cause them; but another clergyman with him was more sceptical. The Rev J. Harper, a Primitive Methodist minister, also heard knocking, and did not believe that there was any shamming on the part of the girl. A doctor who visited believed that she herself did it. Superintendant Stephens, of the county police, went to the cottage with the determination of finding out if there was any deception, and he stood at the foot of the stairs and watched the girl whilst listening to the knocking, but saw nothing suspicious in her conduct and believes that she herself did not do it. One night when two men were in the same room as the girl mysterious knocking was heard. The girl (who looked ill and weary) has been admitted into the infirmary at Salisbury, and the strange sounds at Homington have now ceased, whilst she herself is very much better than at the time of her admission.'

What was actually happening here? In some ways this looks like a typical poltergeist case, and one with some convinced and respectable witnesses. What, though, does the gypsy have to do with it? As far as we can tell, Lydia seems to have become fixated with her for some reason, and this nervous obsession then somehow catalysed the outburst of poltergeist rappings. They may have been sparked by Lydia's actual belief in bewitchment, or this notion may have been imposed on the affair by onlookers after the strange noises began. What we do know is that, when people believe in the power of witches, their fear can indeed turn them into poltergeist agents. This happened in Ireland in 1661, and in Brightling, Sussex sometime before 1691. In both cases, the agents, or 'victims' were young girls.

A peculiar feature of the Homington case is, of course, the knowledge which these ghostly rappings display. These kind of conversations are not uncommon in the history of the poltergeist: they were convincingly reported, for example, by the Wesley family from Epworth Rectory in winter 1716-17. When these rappings appear to display knowledge not available to anyone in the household, we have to assume either that there is an omniscient ghost involved, or that the agent is in fact telepathic, or is gifted with psychic knowledge of the future. In Homington, bizarre as the events were, it may just have been that Lydia already knew all this information, and projected it somehow through the rappings, albeit unconsciously. Notice, too, that as so often the poltergeist phenomena stop when the agent is removed.

Unnatural Animals

Sinister rabbits, a metamorphosing sheep, dogs and cats with eyes of fire, and vampire tabbies… Some of these stories seem to be one more jigsaw piece in that great ghostly puzzle of supernatural hysteria and consequent wild invention which stretches across the nineteenth century. Others, such as the Wish Hounds of Dartmoor and the uncanny rabbits, owe more to longstanding magical traditions. A word of warning before you venture into this occult menagerie. You may by now think yourself pretty hardened to the varied supernatural terrors of the nineteenth century. But it is perhaps time to think again. For you about to meet a bunny which can scare grown men…

to death.

50. A Sea Monster.
Liverpool Mercury, 26 January 1816.

'Alexandria, 9 Dec. The Brig Trim, Capt. Cleveland on her passage from Gibraltar to this port, on the 25th October, in latitude 31 longitude 20, passed a substance in the water, about 25 or 30 foot from the vessel, which from its extraordinary appearance, induced the Captain to tack ship, with a view to examine what it was – the wind being light from the WSW [he] caused the boat to be lowered down, and sent the mate with two men to make discovery. On their return they gave the following description:

"When we came in sight of the fore-mentioned substance, [we] turned the boat and tacked her stern nearly over him, then about four feet under water lying coiled up with its head on the top of the coil – the head being pointed, and about 12 or 14 inches in length, with upper and lower tushes or teeth, appeared from three to four inches outside, the jaws shut within each other, appeared curvely like the tush of a hog, and extremely white. His body had the appearance in size of about three to three and a half feet in circumference, tapering towards the tail – and his colour was of the deepest crimson, and reflected through the water some yards. The boat being to leeward of the reptile, the little wind and sea, while they stood viewing him, drifted it off, about 30 to 40 feet; the mate then concluded to hook him; the noise of the oars at first stroke started him, he threw himself out at his length, with his head towards the boat and came very near, raising himself nearly to the surface of the water, in an attitude of attack. It was judged best to make for the vessel. His length could not have been less than 30 to 40 feet, and we judge him to be in form and appearance like a sea serpent.'

51. The Dogs of Hell.
North Wales Chronicle, 6 April 1847.

'The Abbots Way [on Dartmoor] is the especial haunt of the Wish, or Wisked Hounds - the wildest and most remarkable of the supernatural beings which still linger within the bounds of the old forest of the Dartmoors. The Wish Hounds, as they are called (a name probably connected with the Anglo-Saxon "wicca", a witch) are under the immediate guidance of that mysterious being, whose nature "well may I guess, but dare not tell". In the pauses of the storm, and mingling with the hoarse voices of the rapidly swelling mountain waters, the broken cry of dogs, the shouting of the hunters, the loud blasts of their horns, and the sound of "hoofs thick beating on the hollow hill", are borne onward upon the winds of the forest; and when the dark curtain of mist rolls slowly up over the hillside, they may sometimes be seen to sweep across the moors, rough, swarthy, of huge size, and with fiery sparks shooting from their eyes and nostrils.

It is not safe to leave the door of the house ajar; for in this case they have the power of entering, and have been known to devour sleeping children in the absence of the household. For this reason it is still the custom in some of the wilder parts of Devonshire to place a crust of bread beneath the pillow of the cradle: a charm which perhaps had its origin in the very ancient custom of reserving a certain portion of the consecrated bread of the Eucharist – which, carried by each communicant to his own home, might there be partaken of daily, and was supposed to preserve the house from all evil.

Certain spots on Dartmoor are more commonly haunted by the Wish Hounds than others; and on its borders there are many long narrow lanes, closely overgrown with thorn and hazel, through which they pass in long procession on particular nights – of which St John's Eve is always one. A person who was passing at night over the moors above Withecombe, heard them sweep through the valley below him with a great cry and shouting, and when he reached the highest point of the hill, he saw them pass by, with the "Master" behind - a dark gigantic figure, carrying a long hunting pole at his back, and with a horn slung around his neck. When they reached the ancient earthwork of Hembury Fort – which rises on a high wooded hill above the Dart – the Master blew a great blast upon his horn, and the whole company sank into the earth.

Their appearance, however, is by no means without danger to the beholder; and even the sound of their distant cry among the hills is a forewarning of evil to those who hear it. Not long since, a number of men, with dogs and ferrets, proceeded (on the Sabbath day) to trespass on a large rabbit warren, near the source of the water of Avon; but when they got to a wind hollow in the hillside, the dogs "heard the Wish Hounds", and at once set up a dismal howling. They were cheered on by their masters – but nothing could prevent them running homewards as fast as they could; "and at the end of a fortnight", said the warrener," the dogs were all dead"'.

This last story is impressively specific. The following Welsh case, arguably, is even more so.

"'As R.A. was going to Laugharn town one evening on some business, it being late, her mother dissuaded her from going, telling her that it was late, and she would be benighted; likely she might be terrified by an apparition, which was both seen and heard by many, and by her father among others, at a place called "Pant-y-madog", which was a pit by the side of the lane leading to Laugharn, filled with water and not quite dry in the summer. However, she seemed not to be afraid, and therefore went to Laugharn. On coming back before night (though it was rather dark), she passed by the place, but not without thinking of the apparition. But being a little beyond this pit, in a field where there is a little rill of water, and just going to pass it, having one foot stretched over it, and looking before her, she saw something like a great dog (one of the dogs of hell) coming towards her; being within four or five yards of her, it stopped, sat down, and set up such a scream, so horrible, so loud and so strong, that she thought the earth moved under her, with which she fainted and fell down. She did not awake and go to the next house, which was but the length of one field from the place, until about midnight, having one foot wet in the rill of water which she was going to pass when she saw the apparition.'"

The writer who originally cited this tale was a Welsh Independent minister, Edmund Jones. Jones's tales (published in 1780 as *A Relation of Apparitions of Spirits in the Principality of Wales*) need treating with some caution, given that one of his main aims in assembling his collection was to attack those whose failure to believe in spirits, fairies, ghosts and so forth was also, for him, a failure to believe in God. But it is still worth adding Jones's original closure to the Laugharne tale, which tells us, of the unlucky girl: 'She was very weak that night; and for a long time after a very loud noise would disturb, and sicken her. She owned it was a just punishment for her presumption, and disobeying her good mother's advice.' Clearly, whatever actually happened that night, it had a very real effect on young R.A.

Readers may have noticed that a little bit of cheating went on here, given that these are not exactly newspaper stories about recent events. But they are, I hope you'll agree, a bit too good to leave out. Disappointingly, despite my most rigorous philological investigations, I failed to prove that 'Pant-y-madog' is Welsh for 'panting mad dog'. But be warned, nonetheless.

52. Satan's Tom-Cats.
The Liverpool Mercury, 4 December 1835.

'It will be in the remembrance of our readers that on Sunday morning, the 28th of June last, the body of a poor houseless wretch, called Thomas Parry, nicknamed "the Slasher" from his quarrelsome and drunken habits, was found lying on some timber, in the neighbourhood of Warwick Street, Toxteth Park, under circumstances which left no doubt that a brutal murder had been committed. The body was shockingly mutilated, and the head battered, as if with a hammer … All endeavours to discover the authors of this dreadful outrage have since been unavailing.

Within the last few days a report has been current that the murdered man has "revisited the glimpses of the moon", we presume from the same motive that induced Shakespeare's King of Denmark to leave his prison-house, namely to bring the authors of his death to justice; and great has been the horror, excitement and alarm produced by the report amongst the credulous portion of the community, especially in the neighbourhood which the ghostly visitant is said to have chosen for his peregrinations ... It is reported that the watchman of the district was favoured with the first view, and that it occurred in the following manner: on Sunday se'nnight, about "the witching hour of night", he was going his rounds, and on his passing near the scene of the murder, which is a very lonely spot, nearly in the fields, covered with immense piles of timber, he saw what he took to be a man, busily engaged with a lever in moving the timber. Thinking this rather a curious employment at such an hour, he called out to know what the man was about, when, instead of giving a civil answer, or speaking when spoken to, according to the approved fashion of ordinary ghosts, the figure vanished in a flash of fire, and with it the lever, which, from this circumstance, would appear to have been a ghost likewise. On this awful denouement, the valiant watchman, it is said, remembering the fate of "the Slasher", had all his doubts converted into certainty, fainted away, was found in that state in the morning and conveyed home, where he took to his bed, and was hardly expected to recover from the effects which this supernatural visitation had upon his nerves.

The story spead like wildfire, and crowds of persons have since visited the place nightly in the hope or fear of seeing a similar spectacle. It does not appear that their laudable curiosity has been gratified, though reports innumerable are in circulation on the subject.

According to one of them, no fewer than three clergymen were engaged to send the troubled spirit packing to the Red Sea, an undertaking in which they are said to have failed, simply because the ghost was so unmannerly as not to come to be laid. Probably he has some well-founded objections of his own to the process. Another rumour is, that his ghostship has been seen with a huge balk of timber on his shoulders, in full pursuit of the watchman. Another, that he has been observed picking his teeth with one of the levers which he was accustomed to handle during his earthly pilgrimage; and yet a fourth, that he occasionally indulges himself with driving about in a timber carriage, by four huge tom cats, four in hand, with eyes of fire, and mouths vomiting flame, so that their can be no doubt whatever as to their pedigree'.

53. An Angry Sheep.
Lancaster Gazette, 25 January 1851.

'Between Bolton-le-Sands and Carnforth, on the roadside, is situated a house having the reputation of being haunted, and has ever, within the memory of that oft-quoted personage, "the oldest inhabitant", been known by the inhabitation of the "boggart house". Various are the conjectures respecting the manner in which this lonely dwelling received the distinction; but on one point all agree, that at some time or other it has been the theatre where some "deed of darkness" has been enacted; that "murder most foul" has been committed within its precincts, and the perturbed spirit of the victim is permitted for a time to visit the "pale glimpses of the moon, making night hideous".

Many a one, in passing this dreaded spot, upon hearing the slightest sound, the faintest rustling of the trembling leaves, has felt a curious sensation run down his back and ooze out at his toes, and not a few who had great pretensions to fearlessness, when coming into immediate proximity with the "boggart house", have felt themselves compelled to "whistle to bear their courage up". Numerous are the forms in which this supernatural agent presents itself, sometimes as a headless soldier, a gigantic sheep, or monster goose. Often does his ghostship play fantastic tricks, such as only appertain to the denizens of another and unknown world, such as acting the part of an invisible glazier, taking out panes of glass and throwing them down on the floor without injury etc. For a short time back this ghostship has been better behaved, confining himself within his own "cerements" and never disturbing sublunary mortals with "things above the reaches of their souls".

However, last week the "dobby" again made his appearance, much to the terror of an inoffensive carter who was proceeding on his way to Kendal market. This occurrence has been a rich theme this past week for the gossip-mongers at Bolton, and the neighbourhood, and has been the all-engrossing topic of conversation. The carter to which we have above alluded was on his way to Kendal market, with a load of wheat, shortly after the witching hour of night "when churchyards yawn", and had proceeded as far as the immediate vicinity of the "boggart house", when his horse suddenly stopped and appeared much frightened. On looking to ascertain the cause, he perceived as he imagined a large sheep lying in the middle of the road, towards which he proceeded with the intention of applying his whip to force its removal. He struck, the blow fell upon vacancy, the supposed sheep aroused itself and as with indignity at the insult, swelled out, *as the man affirms* into the size of a house, and then giving him a look of ineffable contempt, flew away in a flame of fire.

The poor carter was petrified, the chattering of his teeth almost rivalled in noise the bone-playing of the celebrated "Jubs", his knees shook, and his legs refused to perform their office. How long he remained in this condition he is unable to state, but the fright had such an effect upon his nerves as to make him seriously unwell, and he has not since recovered the shock. Although we have no faith in these supernatural visitations, it must be admitted that the poor man, from the state he was in, had seen something which dreadfully alarmed him. Perhaps on the previous evening he had been partaking too freely of the "barley bree", and his heated imagination magnified the apparition.'

The oddest mixture, here... If we had only the carter's description of the indignant sheep (sounding uncannily like an ovine version of the Incredible Hulk) this tale would probably rank with the wildest superstitions of the age. As it is, two other details complicate the picture intriguingly. First: even the highly sardonic reporter (who surely was told by his editor, 'pad this one out, would you? the usual hackneyed Shakespeare quotations. whatever') cannot help but feel that the carter (who may well have suffered a nervous breakdown) must have seen *something* terrifying. Second: we have the mysterious 'invisible glazier', allegedly removing panes of glass at the farm and laying them down unharmed. This does sound remarkably like poltergeist behaviour, in which impish chaos often alternates with seemingly impossible levels of control (compare the undamaged furniture and uninjured residents of Beckley Lower Farm in 1857). Boggart House Farm at Station Lane, Barton, is still a working dairy-farm in the present day.

White Rabbits and Witch Rabbits

54. *Morning Post*, 30 September 1829.

'A white cat, belonging to a person residing near the churchyard, Bath, having been seen playing from grave to grave, a report crept into circulation that it was an old witch, who had assumed the form of a rabbit! A council was held at a neighbouring public-house; after several learned and serious debates, it was determined that at midnight the landlord should fire at it with a silver bullet. At twelve o'clock – "that ominous hour when spirits leave their graves!" – the landlord, armed cap-a-pie (accompanied by several others) bravely sallied forth, determined to destroy the poor witch. In a moment puss (as was her usual custom) was seen frisking about the churchyard. [The landlord], with his accustomed bravery, presented, fired, and missed! The affrighted animal sought refuge in a neighbouring house, where these heroes discovered the object of so much alarm. Early the next morning the landlord obtained a white rabbit, and, having placed a pair of ear-rings in its ears, declared it to be the witch he had shot the preceding night. In the course of that and the following day hundreds were seen flocking from all parts of the town to inspect the poor witch; and the landlord reaped a golden harvest from the credulity of the public.'

55. *Morning Post*, 31 January 1849.

'The White Rabbit at Dartmouth.

Dartmouth, like every other town, has had its full share of ghosts, ghost stories, and ghost believers, but for a period of time more than covering the last half century, it has been mysteriously visited by some unearthly being, in an earthly shape of a white rabbit; many of the oldest inhabitants can bear testimony to the fact, that the white rabbit's ghost used regularly, as soon as darkness set in of a night, to take its march from the churchyard down through one or two of the principal streets of the town, gambolling heedlessly along, to the terror of most persons who saw it. Some few bolder than the rest have been known to attempt to capture the intruder; shots have been fired at it, men have given chase, and on more than one occasion the pursuer has securely placed his hat over the prize, but on lifting which the vanished rabbit has made it evident that it was not ordinary flesh and blood. Hundreds of persons used to witness the patrol of this delicate looking ghost, but the honour of capturing it during the last week has fallen on our indefatigable head constable, Hearn. Hearn's story is, that on opening and entering the council chamber on Tuesday morning, he heard very strange noises proceeding from some part of the building; however, there being a good supply of constables' staves close at hand, he armed himself, and, after a long search, discovered and captured, without much resistance, a very large white rabbit. Nearly all the members of the town council visited and saw this animal in the Guildhall the same morning of its capture, and from its singular ancient look, coupled with its lean condition, it was pronounced to be the white rabbit of Dartmouth. The general opinion is, that it must have purposely gone to the Guildhall, with the intention of delivering itself up, to satisfy the ends of justice.'

56. *Trewman's Exeter Flying Post,* 13 November 1851.

'It is rumoured that certain of the people of Ottery have for some time past been nightly engaged in laying a witch which has appeared there in the shape of a white rabbit. At last one of the party, who was armed with a gun, catching a glimpse of the supposed witch fired and killed it. On examination it turned out to be Farmer Channon's white cat.'

57. *Leeds Mercury,* 28 February 1891.

'A more harmless, but scarcely less inexplicable [superstition] is that of the white rabbit, which still lingers in many Yorkshire villages. It is said that whoever sees a white rabbit cross his path at night is doomed to speedy death. The older portion of many village communities believe in this superstition faithfully. I remember a stonemason, a man of fifty or thereabouts, who one moonlight night, went with his grown-up son, a man of 25, to net sparrows in a stack-yard at a village three miles away. Having caught a number of sparrows, they were thinking of returning home when the father suddenly saw a white rabbit scud across his path in the moonlight, and disappear in a lump of thorns which had been placed in one corner of the stack-yard. He and his son both having watched it disappear, attacked the thorns from either side, their dog keeping an eager eye open in the middle. They went carefully into the corner, and found nothing. Neither was there any way by which the white rabbit could have escaped. The father turned pale, said to his son, Well, tis a warning", and set off home at a run. He went straight to bed, never got up again, and died in four days. His family and friends of course believe he was warned; but he probably died of fright.'

Belief in witch-rabbits or hares was impressively widespread and durable – reflecting the idea that witches not only had animal familiars, but could also change themselves into animals of various kinds. Researching traditional beliefs in Country Antrim in Northern Ireland in the late 1930s, H.T.

Browne still heard 'in nearly every district ... of the old dame who changed herself into a hare and sucked the cows' milk, and of course all the shooting at the hare was useless until some bright fellow loaded his gun with a silver sixpence, and that same evening old Mrs So-and-so was carried into the house with a bullet wound in her leg'. Variants on this tale involved the claim that, ever after, Mrs X was seen to limp on that leg (and I'm not one to goosip, as ye know, but they do say...). In light of these beliefs, we can see how the landlord's stratagem with those rabbit ear-rings made pretty sinister sense to people in Bath in 1829.

Notice that three of these four cases occur in the south-west of England. Almost eighty years after Farmer Channon's poor puss bit the dust, one M.P. Watkin was holidaying near Ottery St Mary, where his eighty year old great-aunt, Miss Cornish, had lived all her life. Calling in on her for tea one day, Watkin mentioned that he had tried unsuccessfully to shoot some peculiarly dark-coloured rabbits which he had seen in her fields. Visibly shocked, Miss Cornish replied, "But my dear, nobody shoots those", before going on to explain that "they might be witches". The fact that these uncanny bunnies had changed their colour so notably since Victorian days seems only to confirm their dubious status. Given the great ease with which so many people combined religious and magical beliefs in the past, it is interesting to find that the evidently wealthy Miss Cornish was daughter of Ottery's sometime local vicar.[5]

Vampire Cats

58. *Freeman's Journal*, 31 October 1882.

'The question whether cats can kill children by sucking their breath has always been a grave matter of discussion between all the old women who believe it and the doctors who do not believe it, or at least deny that there is any reason for believing it. A Pittsburgh mother the other day went up to the bedroom and found her infant child dead, with a big cat sitting on its breast. The lower portion of the child's face and a part of the neck were discoloured, the tongue swollen and the lips black. The cat had been kicked out of the room several times. The father, mother, and all the neighbours were sure the cat had killed it by sucking its breath; but the doctor said there were no authenticated cases of the kind. Cats are fond of babies, and will often put their noses to the little ones' mouths, attracted probably by the smell of milk. It would be impossible for a cat to stop a child's breath, and "as for sucking it, it is absurd". He conjectured that the child died from convulsions or strangulation'.

The Morning Post, 3 October 1890.

Chicago Oct 2. 'A coroner's inquest was held yesterday upon the body of the infant child of a Mrs Woydas. The evidence went to prove that the child had been killed by having its breath sucked by a cat, and a verdict to that effect was rendered'.

59. 'Killed by a Cat's Breath'.

Hampshire Telegraph, 9 June 1894.

'Dr Livingstone records in his Life that once, in Africa, he was seized by a lion, who broke his arm. The crunching of the broken limb, however, gave him no pain, so benumbed were his senses by the animal's breath. All the *felidae* possess poisonous breaths, intended by nature to act as an anaesthetic on their prey. The truth of this statement can be easily realised by inhaling a cat's breath, or if one watches pussy playing with a mouse they will discover that the victim is stupefied, as if by chloroform. Medical records conclusively prove that small children have died through inhaling the cat's breath. The animal, attracted by the soft bed and warm body of the sleeping child, sits down on the chest of the infant. Its weight impedes respiration, its breath anaesthetises the child, and death follows.'

60. 'Can Cats Suffocate Children?'

Hampshire Telegraph and Sussex Chronicle, 29 August 1896.

'In the course of a chat with a journalist a physician of experience said:

"Most people will ridicule the idea that cats are harmful to the health of young children, and laugh away the old-fashioned notion that they sometimes sucked away their breath as an old-wife's superstition. But I have very good evidence to show that this really *does* occur now and again. Mothers have brought me their babies in such an exhausted condition as could only have been explained by some such cause, and have pointed out the marks where the cat's lips have been attached. In one case a lady assured me that she had actually watched for some minutes a young kitten crawling into the cradle, and had seen it fasten its teeth over the infant's mouth. The cause of the terribly dangerous practice is a very simple one. The young and suckling kitten smells the milk round the lips of the little one, and by instinct desires to share it. She finds the sensation of inhaling the warm, moist, milky breath a pleasant one, and hangs on til the poor child is suffocated. Of course only very young cats who can be attracted by milk will do this, but adult animals are dangerous too, in the nursery. They like the warmth and comfort of the cot, and (in the absence of a careless nurse) will crawl in and stretch themselves right across the poor baby's body. Doubtless many of the mysterious deaths of infants ... are due to the unsuspected kitten that gambols so innocently round the foot of the cot'.

Magic

One of the strangest lessons of studying popular beliefs is this: for most people, for most of history, there was nothing but magic. Religion was all very well, but what actually went on in the heads of those ordinary, often illiterate men and women who obediently attended church every Sunday could be a matter of bewilderment or outrage to educated Christians. Back in the time of James I, the Puritan minister William Pemble recalled 'a dying man of sixty who had attended church several times a week throughout his lifetime'. '"Being demanded [on his deathbed] what he thought of God, he answers that he was a good old man; and what of Christ, that he was a towardly young youth; and of his soul, that it was a great bone in his body; and what should become of his soul after he was dead, that if he had done well he should be put into a pleasant green meadow..."'.[6]

Listening to certain Greeks, interviewed in the 1960s, who felt that heaven was a village where the most pious person had the best house, we can well imagine that popular attitudes to religion did not change that much between the seventeenth and nineteenth centuries. It was also in Greece that Patrick Leigh Fermor encountered church paintings from which the plaster eyes of saints had been scraped away to make love potions or medicines. And this brings us to perhaps the most important link between religion and magic for most ordinary people. Quite simply, both should be useful. They should protect you, or solve any problems which befell you, your family, your animals or your crops. Some magic you could do yourself, as we have seen all too memorably in the case of those witch-cuttings. In other cases, you went to a reputed professional for help: possibly another witch, possibly a cunning-man or woman. But whatever your choice, you were after practical concrete results, and you did not expect to have to spend years at Hogwarts, learn Latin, or make compacts with the Devil to get them. As we saw in the case of Mary Bateman and the Perigos, some cunning folk were outright fraudsters. But others probably believed in what they did, however far-fetched it might now seem to us.

61. A Magic Bottle.

Lancaster Gazette, 12 May 1804.

'A singular, yet melancholy accident lately happened at Blackshaw, near Stansfield, Yorkshire. The following are the particulars, which plainly demonstrate that the age of *superstition* is not yet passed. An aged man of the name of Robert Sutcliff, a weaver, possessed the silly idea that his house was troubled by a witch or devil, by whose supernatural agency, and nightly excursions, the clothes of his family were cut, the threads broke in his looms, and several other injuries committed.

He at length applied to a person of the name of John Hepworth, near the Cock and Bottle Inn, in Bradford, a kind of fortune-teller, for his assistance to deliver him from the power of this mysterious tormentor! The pretended Exorciser went in consequence to the haunted house, where he procured a large *iron bottle*, into which he poured human blood, previously drawn from the arm of a boy – a quantity of hair, with other materials, and after a few incantations, he corked the bottle well up, and carefully deposited the same in the middle of a hot fire. In a short time the bottle burst with a terrible explosion – the windows of the house were driven out, and a great part of the chimney fell down. It is melancholy, however, to relate, that the poor unfortunate old man, who had been repeatedly importuned to leave the room, but had strenuously persisted in refusing, received a dreadful wound by the bursting of the bottle, and died a few days afterwards.'

The reasons for filing this one under 'Magic' are probably obvious enough. But the notion that Sutcliff's fears were based purely on a 'silly idea' was evidently misguided, as the cutting or slashing of clothes is in fact a well-known trait of certain poltergeists (Geoff Holder, for example, found that it featured in 3% of 134 Scottish poltergeist cases). This then makes us wonder: who was the agent? Although Sutcliff was said to be 'an aged man', reference to 'his family' implies more than just a wife – it seems that some of his children were still in the house, and at least young enough to act as the focal point of these uncanny activities. This was a tragedy, certainly; but a more complicated one than we might at first think.

62. Blood Magic.
The Morning Post, 22 December 1836.

On 7 Dec 1835 'a little after two o'clock in the morning, the watchman at an abattoir in Marseilles observed something that looked white on the pavement close to the door of the charity hospital; and on examining it closely he found it to be a corpse. At the same moment three persons, who appear to have been waiting at the corner of the street, ran away and were not overtaken.

The watchman called for assistance, and two of the night patrol having come up the body was ascertained to be that of a quack, named Antoine Arnaud. The hands and feet were tied together, but the clothes were not removed; and the head was covered with several handkerchiefs that served to conceal a large wound in the throat.

At the Hotel Dieu it was found that the body had been opened by a longitudinal incision from the breast, which had been subsequently sewn up. The wound in the throat had divided several arteries, and must have caused death from excessive bleeding, though no blood was anywhere visible. The medical men were astonished to see that the intestines, the heart, the liver and the various organs had been apparently torn from their places, and afterwards crammed into the pectoral and abdominal cavities, without any care or proper arrangement. Notwithstanding the rough manner in which they had been handled, however, all the organs were entire, except the liver, of which nearly the half had been taken away.'

A police investigation revealed 'that the deceased had been some years resident at Marseilles, where he carried on the double profession of day labourer and quack doctor. It seems that he took the greatest and most disinterested care of his patients, for it could not be discovered that he ever received money, except in a solitary instance, when 1500 francs had been given to him by a man in better circumstances than the persons who usually employed him. After a few inquiries there was good ground for believing that he had fallen a victim to a system prescribed by himself. His system of medicine was decidedly the most extraordinary ever heard of. Whenever a patient applied, he gave the following directions: " I am about to take a soporific, and when I am asleep you will pierce my neck with a knife (*Vous me plongerez un couteau dans le col*). The blood issuing from the wound will entirely cure your disorder."

The police at length, after having arrested and examined several persons against whom there appeared to be no proof, traced the house in which the deceased had last been seen alive. It belonged to a young woman named Camille Viacca, who had been for some time under his care. A long series of circumstantial, but seemingly decisive, evidence, left no room to doubt that to the too-faithful adherence to his own prescription by this woman and one of her friends the death of Arnaud must be attributed; and the case was brought before the regular tribunals.

But here an unexpected difficulty arose. Notwithstanding the skill of the public prosecutor it was exceedingly puzzling to know how to frame the indictment. Homicide had clearly been committed, but evidently without "malice aforethought". The death of the practitioner was obviously the result of his own instructions; and his liver had evidently been cut out for the purpose of preserving his life.

An immense crowd was present at the trial, when several witnesses proved the directions given by the deceased. M. Lieutaud, acting for the Procureur-General, left the case entirely in the hands of the jury, who discharged the prisoners.'

63. Death by Holy Water.
Bell's Life in London and Sporting Chronicle, 16 March 1834.

'A few days ago the body of a man, stark naked and quite dead, was found in a sitting posture immersed in the water of St Winifred's Well, at Holywell in Wales. It appears that the deceased, respecting whom nothing is known, was a pilgrim to Holywell, for the purpose of bathing in the far-famed well, for the cure of some real or imaginary ailment and that, nothing daunted by the coolness of the weather, he stripped off his clothes, and took his seat in the well, either late on Sunday evening, or early on the morning of Monday. The consequence has been already described. A coroner's inquest has been held on the body, and a verdict of "Found Dead" returned. When found, he had a string of beads round his neck, with a crucifix attached to it.'

64. Black Cat Cocktail.
Preston Guardian, 1 May 1847.

'A few days ago a single man, from twenty to thirty years of age, named Robert Ashworth, residing at Marland, Castleton, went to a woman named Alice Platt, alias Crap, Brick Croft, near Toad Lane, who is said to be a fortune teller, and a seller of charms, spells, and small medicine, in the hope of being cured of epilpetic fits, with which he has been afflicted for many years. The following is the remedy which she prescribed: at the full moon, he was to procure a black tom cat, which he was to put in a reticule. He was then to draw out its tail, which he was to cut at the fourth joint. He was directed to catch thirty drops of blood, and add about a wine glass of the best Hollands' gin, and to drink the mixture at midnight, on the same day the moon is full. Immediately after taking the medicine he was to go to bed, to place a sealed paper, which she gave him, under his head, and not to rise until six o' clock in the morning. The woman, who is about fifty years of age, and wears a man's old jacket, assured the young man that if he would follow her directions, and repeat the Lord's prayer when he rose in the morning, he would never have fits again. Her fee would only be one shilling. Last week the man was promised a black male cat, and he persists in saying he will try the remedy at the next full moon.'

This, by the way, was only a mildly desperate remedy for epilepsy. Another longstanding one involved drinking fresh human blood at an execution scaffold (see *Mummies, Cannibals and Vampires* for details). Or, as Leo Kanner notes, if you were an epileptic man you could get yourself castrated (something still being reported around 1850, just three years after Ashworth's tale). You could eat the testicles of a bear, pulverised camel's brain, a young dog, maggots from a rotting sheep's nose, or earthworms during coitus (yours, not theirs). You could drink the urine of a black horse, the blood of your father or mother, or wine with woodlice in it.

Cat's blood, anyone?

65. European Voodoo.
Bradford Observer, 31 Dec 1857.

'We have now to record a novel method of terrifying the proprietor of the soil. Nothing less than "witchery" and incantations; he is to be spell-bound, nay, his death is to be compassed by witchcraft. We are telling no idle tale. A respectable gentleman has sent us the following particulars respecting an occurrence which will create more than ordinary surprise, and which lately took place in the parish of Ballinakill, barony of Leitrim, and the County of Galway: "a gentleman in this parish let his lands in the famine times at the low figure of 12s per acre. Twelve months ago, he served his tenants with notices that he would increase the rent of his lands from November, 1856, otherwise he would give each tenant three months' rent for leaving it.

All the time they held it at this low figure, they never laid out one shilling on improvements – a few complied and paid the increase of rent. The others were served with notices to quit a few days ago, and also ejectments for the next session. While this was being done, they got out two querns, gathered together men, women, and children to the highest hill, [taking] two effigies of straw – one for their landlord, the other for his bailiff; then they commenced to grind, shouting the Irish cry and clapping their hands. They ground in the devil's name, washing the effigies in the river in the devil's name – got a stretcher and sheets and had a regular funeral procession to one of the houses; held a wake there, and had plenty of pipes and tobacco. They buried the imaginary corpses secretly some time in the night. If the place was known they think the charm would not take effect. In their superstitious minds they believe when the effigies begin to rot the parties ground (ie, the landlord and bailiff) will get sick and will eventually die'.

Anyone who thinks that European voodoo was peculiarly Irish might be interested to know that the composer and pacifist Ronald Duncan found a Widow Yelston actively sticking pins into dolls of her neighbours in North Devon one winter. It seemed to work. The date was the late 1940s.

66. Superstition in Switzerland.
The Star, 1 November 1883.

'An extraordinary instance of superstition is reported from the Swiss village of St Fiden, in the Canton of St

Gall. The keeper of the cemetery remarked that one particular tombstone was thrown to the ground every night, though he put it back in the perpendicular position every morning. The inhabitants of the village, who are very credulous, believed that it must be the work of the "spirits", but the solution of the mystery was, as may be imagined, a natural one. It seems that three men living in the village had formed an association for the purpose of "raising" money after a receipt which they had discovered in a work on sorcery by Albertus Magnus.

They believed that by throwing down a tombstone at midnight several times in succession, depositing under it 32 five franc pieces, and reciting certain incantations, the 32 pieces would be converted into 5 million francs. After hiding the money they retired to a hut away from the village, and remained there a week without clothes, eating but bread, and drinking nothing but water. This they thought would propitiate the "spirit of Hisis". Two of the three men were discovered in this hut in a state of semi-starvation; but the third, being of a more practical turn, finding that the miraculous multiplication was not effected, quietly took up the 32 pieces of silver, and disappeared with them. His two companions still believe that the miracle will take place if they continue their incantations.'

Readers may well be wondering why the Catholic Saint, Albertus Magnus (c.1206-1280), should take such an interest in the Egyptian deity, Isis. The answer is that he almost certainly did not; there was a great tradition of crediting recipes to Magnus, thought by some to be the greatest scientist of his day. Back in the sixteenth century one of these formulae was 'a most precious water' of distilled human blood, believed able to raise the sick from their deathbeds.

67. The Key and the Bible.
The York Herald, 12 February 1887.

'A case recently investigated in the Birmingham police court reveals an amount of superstition almost incredible. Maria Williams, the wife of a brass caster, summoned Mary Ann Ling, a neighbour, for assaulting her, and there was a cross-summons by Ling against Williams for assault. It appears that on the day named Ling missed a sum of money, and Williams was accused of the theft. Other neighbours were called in, and decided that the question of Mrs Williams's guilt or innocence should be put to the test of "trial by ordeal". The ordeal consisted in suspending a bible by means of worsted [thread], and making it rotate by twisting the worsted round a key in the manner sometimes adopted in poor families for roasting. The jury of matrons and the parties to the dispute arranged themselves in a semi-circle in front of the dangling book, having agreed that whomsoever the bible pointed to when it finished rotating should be considered guilty. In the result the book pointed to Mrs Williams, and thereupon ensued a resort to violence, which resulted in Mrs Ling being fined 5s and costs or seven days, the cross-summons being dismissed'.

Versions of this ritual (which perfectly typifies the magical use so many people made of religion) went back hundreds of years. We can suspect that the trick was attempted in some areas well into the twentieth century.

68. 'An Amazing Story'.
The Leicester Chronicle, 26 August 1893.

'The following amazing story is told in a French provincial journal, and what is more amazing still is that its truth is vouched for a by a person in whom the editor has sufficient faith to print it. It reads like a brain-sick perversion of Elsie Venner. There is a young girl, called Sophie Walder - it is not said where she lives – who is put into a trance by her father. She wears a necklace of gold shaped like a serpent, which her father then takes off, twisting round her neck in its place a real serpent. The reptile then puts its head to the girl's mouth, whereupon she is seized with a sort of frenzy, displaying all symptoms attributed to the Delphic priestesses. After this she grows calm again, and her father lays bare her neck and traces on the skin with a blunt piece of iron any question the bystanders ask. In a few minutes the letters are visible. Then the serpent begins to write the answer with its tail, which hangs down the girl's back, and again, after a few minutes, the writing is seen on the skin. Recently the question of was, "How many Popes will there be after Leo XIII?" and the answer came, "Nine – after that I shall reign!" This exhibition is called a demoniacal manifestation.'

In Oliver Wendell Homes's 1861 novel, *Elsie Venner: A Romance of Destiny*, the heroine becomes half-woman, half-snake, apparently due to her mother's having been bitten by a rattlesnake during pregnancy. Readers may or may not be alarmed to know that Francis, elected Pope in 2013, is indeed the ninth Pope to follow Leo XIII – which perhaps raises the question: just *who* is "I"?

Corpse Magic

A few words in advance here, as this topic is so strange that many readers may otherwise get quite lost in the uncanny lights and shadows into which we are about to descend. For centuries, a startling number of people believed that you could render yourself invisible by use of a human hand lit as a torch, or by a candle made from human fat. The first was often known as The Hand of Glory, and one of these can still be seen in the Whitby Museum in Yorkshire. The latter were called 'thieves' candles'. In the second case, desire to get one of these candles led a number of theives to become murderers. It was said that once lighted, the Hand of Glory could never be extinguished save with milk. Notice that whilst this magic is rather blacker than what we have seen above, it also follows the same surprisingly mundane general rule: you do it, not out of any particular love of evil, but because it is *useful* to your and your accomplices.

69. It Could be Vous...

The Morning Post, 8 July 1819.

'A violation of the sacred rites of sepulture has recently been committed by an association of several individuals, linked together by a superstition so gross, and for a purpose so horribly ridiculous, that it will scarcely be believed to have taken place in a country that boasts superior civilisation to the rest of the nations of the earth. The authors of this profanation, after having introduced themselves by night into the cemetery of the Commune of Neyron (Arrondissement of Trevoux, in the departement of the Ain), opened the tomb of the Sieur Antoine Quequet, late Mayor of that commune. They then cut the head off the dead body, and *boiled it for more than an hour in a pot*, in the hope that, after this operation, the head would point out to them the good numbers in the Lottery. The guilty persons are all known, and have been indicted before the correctional police at Trevoux.'

70. The Hand of a Murderer.

The Dundee Courier and Argus, 10 April 1863.

'We stated in our Tuesday's impression that the convict Carter had been executed at Warwick on Monday, for having murdered his sweetheart by shooting her through the back. We now learn that amongst the crowd was an old woman who had brought her daughter over from Tackbrook, and was most persistent in her application at the porter's lodge to see the governor, to obtain his permission for the dead man's hand to be passed across the throat of the girl, who is suffering from a large and unsightly wen. It is an old superstition that the touch of a murderer's hand will cure this disfigurement; but it is almost needless to state that the Governor would not grant the unseemly request.'

71. The Hand of Glory.
Aberdeen Weekly Journal, 3 October 1879.

'One evening between the years 1790 and 1800, a traveller, dressed in woman's clothes, arrived at the Old Spital Inn, the place where the mail-coach changed horses, in High Spital on Bowes Moor. The traveller begged to stay all night, but to go away so early in the morning, that if a mouthful of food were set ready for breakfast, the family need not be disturbed by her departure. The people of the house, however, arranged that a servant-maid should sit up till the stranger was out of the premises, and then went to bed themselves. The girl lay down for a nap on the long settle by the fire; but taking a good look at the traveller first she espied a pair of trousers peeping out from under the gown. All inclination for sleep was gone now; however, with great self-command, she feigned it, closed her eyes, and began to snore. On this the traveller got up, pulled out of his pocket a dead man's hand, fitted a candle to it, lighted the candle, and passed the hand and candle several times before the girl's face, saying as he did so, "Let those who are asleep be asleep, and let those who are awake be awake". This done he placed the light on the table, opened the outer door, went down two or three of the steps which led from the house to the road, and began to whistle for his companions.

The girl ... now jumped up, rushed behind the ruffian, and pushed him down the steps. She then shut the door, locked it, and ran upstairs to try and wake the rest of the family, but all to no purpose – calling, shouting, and shaking, were alike in vain. The poor girl was in despair, for she heard the traveller and his comrades outside the house; so she ran down again, seized a bowl of blue or skimmed milk, and threw it over the hand and candle; after which she went upstairs again, and awoke the sleepers without any difficulty. The landlord's son went to the window, and asked the travellers what they wanted. They answered that if the dead man's hand were but given them, they would go away quietly and do no harm to anyone. This he refused, however, and fired among them. His shot must have taken effect, for in the morning stains of blood were traced to a considerable distance'.

The High Spital case was related in spring 1861 by an old woman, Bella Parkin, living near High Spital. This old woman was a surviving daughter of the servant girl in the tale – one which we will smuggle into our Century, on the grounds that it may have occurred as late as 1800.

72. Thieves' Ointment.
North Eastern Daily Gazette, 4 August 1888.

'Superstition has much to be answerable for in respect to the horrible deeds committed in its name. Few of them, however, can exceed in horror the one brought to our notice as having lately been perpetrated in an out of the way spot of Russia named Scheberschin. A short time after the burial of a much-esteemed Jewish inhabitant of the place his grave was found open. A little distance off lay his skeleton from which every scrap of flesh had been removed. This terrible discovery naturally caused the utmost consternation in the locality, and the enquiry which was set on foot resulted in the authorship of this resulting deed being traced to two men of evil reputations. They ultimately confessed that, with the flesh cut away from the corpse, they hoped to make an ointment, which would have the power of making invisible those who rubbed their bodies with it. Whence this superstitious belief arose is not known; but the miscreants intended to put the powers of the ointment to the test, so as to commit burglaries with impunity'.

Interestingly, this offers us a curious fusion between the more common use of 'thieves' candles' and early modern beliefs surrounding witches. In around 1615, Thomas Middleton, the playwright who adapted Shakespeare's *Macbeth*, composed his own play, *The Witch*. Here we find Hecate 'giving the dead body of a child' to her assistant Stadlin, with the instructions

Boil it well; preserve the fat:
You know 'tis precious to transfer
Our 'nointed flesh into the air,
In moonlight nights, o'er steeple tops.

As in Russia centuries later, the idea is to anoint one's flesh (not, as often said of witches, just the broomstick). Whether the result is flight or invisibility, corpse magic is clearly common to both scenarios.

73. A Whitechapel Murder in Russia.

The Pall Mall Gazette, 24 November 1888.

'A brutal murder, writes our St Petersburg correspondent, has just been committed in the south of Russia which bears one or two points of resemblance to the Whitechapel murders [of Jack the Ripper] ... A peasant girl was found lying dead in a wood near Graivoron (government of Kursk), with evident signs of having been brutally murdered. Moreover certain portions of the body were missing. For several days all efforts to find the murderers were unavailing. No one was even suspected. Soon afterwards, however, a robbery was committed in the village, and suspicion fell on two peasants who were at once arrested. On their rooms being searched a handkerchief was found in which something in the nature of tallow - extracted from human fat – was carefully rolled up. The mother of the murdered girl recognized the handkerchief as her daughter's, and the mystery was soon cleared up.

    The prisoners at once confessed and related the history of the crime in all its details. The hand of a corpse, or even the finger, or a candle made of human fat, is firmly believed by the lower classes throughout the length and breadth of Russia to render the thief who possesses it safe from detection; and as there are many thieves in Russia desirous of pursuing their occupations with impunity, the demand for these objects is considerable. These two peasants resolved to procure some "magic candles" before entering on a series of predatory expeditions. They at first fixed on a peasant as their victim, but when they came to where he was working alone they found him with an axe in his hand, and knowing him to be a strong man they thought it wise to choose another victim. An abnormally stout priest was accordingly fixed upon, but when they called upon him he was away, administering the sacraments to a dying man. They then espied this healthy peasant girl, followed her to the wood, despatched her, and removed certain parts of the body, which they afterwards boiled. They are now under an unusually strong guard, and their trial will take place in a few weeks'.

74. Superstition in Russia.
Blackburn Standard, 22 August 1891.

'A few days ago a terrible crime, the result of an old popular superstition, took place in a small village in the Government of Saratoff. A young child belonging to one of the peasants was found to be missing. An hour after, the body of the missing child was discovered terribly mangled and with its throat cut. The police found that the crime had been perpetrated by an old soldier, who had murdered the child and eaten its heart, under the impression that the heart of an infant would cure him of a disease he had suffered from many years.'

Apparitions

As we all know, ghosts are unruly creatures. Not the least disorderly thing about them is their failure to be easily boxed up into neat categories, where we could very easily separate out ghostly poltergeists from ghostly apparitions. Accordingly, in what follows here we often find elements of typical poltergeist behaviour. But apparitions are distinctive in one interesting way. Simply, they are rare. I have now read or heard around five hundred poltergeist cases, and even in instances where there is evidence of some kind of genuine ghostly personality, it is very unusual to see anything. There again, there are enough credible reports of apparitions to give us something like the beginnings of a rough physics of these things. Once again, they seem to obey certain kinds of laws, as you will see below.

75. 'A Ghost in Cambridge'.
The Morning Post, 12 August 1841.

'The inhabitants of Sidney Sussex College Lodge have lately been alarmed by a supernatural visitation of a very awful description. The following are, as far as we can learn, the circumstances of this extraordinary affair. On Friday night last, about the dread hour of midnight, the nurserymaids, who were about returning to rest, were terrified by hearing several strange and mysterious noises; the sounds appeared to proceed from the staircase; presently they ceased, and the door of the nursery was slowly opened, and a figure of tall and unnatural proportions presented itself before the horror-struck maids. The appearance had a head white and ghastly, long legs, also white, but the body was distinguished only by a dim outline. The body was a shadow – it was a thing of head and legs. The affrighted maids rushed shrieking from the room – the lodge was aroused – the police were called in, but no trace of the apparition was visible, unless a curious odour which perfumed the apartment might be considered so. Next morning a precognition was made by Mr Skrine and Captain Purchase, two of our magistrates, but nothing was discovered. The affair remains shrouded in mystery.'

Like many other sightings of ghostly apparitions, this one reminds us of a key question in the long shadowy history of spectral appearances. Why do we not see ghosts *all the time*? One possible answer is that some form of earthly or human energy is required to let them manifest to the living. This might explain why an otherwise warm room suddenly feels cold during a ghost sighting; and may also be connected to the numerous children and teenagers found central to poltergeist outbreaks, given the potent, often unstable energy of the young and especially the adolescent.

This sense of necessary energy then leads us onto cases in which there seems to be only enough energy to reveal either a shadow-figure, or an incomplete person. During a remarkable haunting at Peterhouse College in Cambridge in 1997, the first sighting of the ghost involved a shadow figure, while a second, some months later, looked initially like an ordinary person – so much so that it was briefly taken for Max Perrutz, a fellow of the College. Meanwhile, back in the 1960s at Washington University's Whittemore House, St Louis, a woman named Myrna, after hearing unexplained footsteps outside her office for some time, rushed out one day to confront the supposed prankster: 'she found herself staring at a man with grey hair and a beard, wearing a red plaid shirt. She was sure the man was flesh and blood, until she looked below his belt. There was nothing below his waist. He was just a torso floating above the carpet. Then he vanished.'

76. Seeing is Believing.
Freeman's Journal, 24 August 1841.

'A very singular circumstance occurred on board the Victory on Friday night last. Two marines (Corporal Wiltshire and Private Newton) on duty, during the midwatch on the main-deck, were passing the last quarter of their watch (a quarter to twelve) by telling tales of ghosts etc, and amidst others related that a policeman ... a few days since was nearly frightened to death by the appearance of a marine on board the Princess Charlotte (which was paid off about a fortnight ago), and which marine it is asserted, was killed on board her at Jean D'Acre. Newton, who was an attentive auditor, declared that he "never could nor would believe in ghosts, and that if even his father had said that he ever saw one, he should set him down as a liar".

No sooner had he spoken than, turning down the deck to walk towards the beef-hatch, he was all at once alarmed by beholding an officer in full naval uniform at a short distance from him, and as it appeared to him, supported by two old sailors, dressed in the fashion of the late wars – to wit, a long pigtail, with all the etc appertaining to an old tar's costume, and with what likewise looked to be hatchets with them. This so alarmed him, that turning to his comrade, Corporal Newton, he exclaimed, "For God's sake, Newton, what is that?" Newton instantly turned and beheld the same, and taking hold of his lantern walked towards the group, when they slowly moved away, and he followed them, when they suddenly vanished near the water-tank. This made Newton's "hair move his cap up" (to use his own expression) and they immediately reported it to the officer of the watch, and the next day to the captain and first lieutenant.

The men are both very steady and credible, and declare most positively that they did see what they related, and they certainly do seem impressed with the belief that it was so.'

By 1841 The Victory, sometime flagship of Lord Nelson at the Battle of Trafalgar, was moored at Portsmouth. The Battle of St Jean D'Acre (La Rochelle, France) had been fought just a few months' before the sighting, on 3 November 1840. Here, as so often, more than one person sees the exact same apparition.

77. A Tall Dark Man.
Liverpool Mercury, 8 May 1857.

'Considerable excitement has prevailed for several days at Beckley, in this county, and the adjoining villages, occasioned by a report ... that a "ghost" had taken up its quarters, at a farmhouse known as Beckley Lower Farm, in the occupation of Mr Chapman. Such was the rapidity with which the rumour flew, and such was the eagerness manifested to obtain a sight of the "haunted house" (a lone farmhouse lying in a hollow, about a mile to the east of Beckley, and six miles from Oxford) that on Friday and Saturday several hundred – and on Sunday it is computed that no less than a thousand – persons of all classes of society made a journey to the farm to gratify their curiosity. Of course the reports in circulation have been many and varied ... but the following facts may be relied on as coming from "an authentic source":

"About the middle of last week Mr Chapman had occasion to go from home, leaving at the house his wife, a female visitor, a servant girl, and four young children. Soon after he had gone, scenes of an extraordinary character commenced. Pieces of the ceiling in every room in the house fell down, making a noise like thunder; brick after brick came rattling down the chimney; tiles fell off the roof, and all this without any apparent human agency. About half the windows in the house are broken; stones, pieces of tile and plaster were thrown through them from without with such force as to break in the leaden frames. And all this went on in the open day, one peculiar characteristic of his ghostship which distinguished him from the generality of his fraternity being his invariable quietness during the "witching hours of night" when, according to popular belief, ghosts delight in indulging their wanton sports.

During the whole of these terrible scenes the females displayed a courage and presence of mind truly praiseworthy ... At each succeeding smash of the windows a most rigid search was instituted by them throughout the grounds adjoining the house, to discover the perpetrator of the mischief, but always without success. One extraordinary circumstance was, we are told, that whenever the bricks or plaster fell on the property of the occupier, the articles of furniture sustained no damage; nor did the inmates of the house receive any injury, with the exception of the servant, who had a trifling bruise on the forehead, occasioned by the falling of a piece of the ceiling in one of the rooms.

Matters continued in this state til Monday last, during the whole of which time not even a momentary glimpse of the "ghost" could be obtained. On the morning of that day, however, the servant, who had been engaged in her domestic duties in the upper part of the house, came rushing downstairs pale with terror, and fell fainting with fright. As soon as she had sufficiently recovered to give an explanation, she said she had encountered a "tall dark man" on the landing of the stairs, and although closely questioned and told that she must have been deceived, she adhered to her statement. All the rooms in the house were immediately examined by the men employed on the farm, but the supernatural intruder was nowhere to be found ... The effect of the sight of the "tall dark man" on the servant girl was such that she could not be induced to remain any longer in the house, and she accordingly left the same day. Whether his ghostship found that his lodgings were getting too warm to be comfortable we cannot say, but it is certain that he has not since been heard of, and the destruction of property of which, of course, he was the author, has ceased from that day. These are simply the facts of the case as we heard them from an inmate of the farm, who kindly volunteered the statement for our information, and we lay them before our readers, leaving them to form their own opinion as to the amount of faith to be placed in them.

The Lower Farm, which is a very old one, has, for nearly a century been associated with many tales of a supernatural character – one of which, credulously believed by many of the labouring classes at the present day, is to the effect that a former tenant of the farm made an agreement with his Satanic Majesty, Nicholas the elder, by which he sold himself for a certain sum of money. A little wood, to the east of the farm, is pointed out, to the inquiring visitor, as the place in which the agreement was drawn up, and to which the tenant was wont to repair to receive payment of his wages. It is added, however, that the "laying" of the "evil spirit" was effectually performed, and that the old man, by always carrying a Bible in his pocket, eluded fulfilling his share of the bargain. Certainly this speaks volumes for the enlightenment of the nineteenth century!'

This is of course in many respects a classic poltergeist case. The combination of violence with lack of damage to property or people is found over and over again in poltergeist incidents spanning centuries. Moreover, the servant girl is almost certainly the unwitting agent for the poltergeist. She is the right kind of age; and the events stop when she leaves. And she probably was telling the truth about the apparition – for which reason I have included the story here, rather than in our Poltergeist chapter.

78. The Ghost On-board HMS Asp.

The Hampshire Advertiser, 1 February 1868.

Letter to the editor of the Pembroke Dock and Tenby Gazette:
'Sir – I shall feel obliged by you inserting in your next impression an account of a "Ghost" which has been seen on board HM Ship, Asp, from 1850 to 1857. The account is in the handwriting of Captain Alldridge, RN, who was in command of that ship at the time...
The MS was sent to me by a gentleman residing at Exeter, whose name I will give to anyone wishing to know it, with a request that I should investigate the matter and supply him with any information I might be able to gain in connexion with this most mysterious tale.

I am, Sir, your obedient servant,

C. Douglas'
Vicarage, Pembroke, 21 January 1868.

Alldridge's letter follows.

'My Dear Sir, I herewith readily comply with your request as far as I am able respecting the unaccountable apparition on board my ship, call it ghost or what you will, still it is a fact that I relate, and much as I was and am a sceptic in ghost stories, I must confess myself staggered and completely at a loss to account for what actually did occur, and never could be accounted for.

Having retired from active service for some years I am unable to recollect dates, but will, as far as I can remember, give them.

In the year 1850 the Asp was given by the Admiralty as a surveying vessel, and on taking possession the Superintendent of the dockyard jokingly remarked, "Do you know, sir, your ship is said to be haunted, and I don't know if you will be able to get the dockyard men to work on her." I of course smiled and said, "Ah, never mind, sir, I don't care for ghosts, and daresay I shall get her all to rights fast enough." I determined in my own mind not to mention a syllable about a ghost to any one; but strange to say, before the shipwrights had been at work a week they begged me to give the vessel up and have nothing more to do with her; that she was haunted, and nothing but ill luck would attend her, and the suchlike! However, the vessel left the dockyard, and arrived safely in the River Dee, where her labours were to commence.

After my day's work was over I generally read a book after tea, or one of my officers would read aloud to me (he is now Master of the Majicienne) and on such occasions he would meet with continued interruption from some strange noises in the after (or ladies') cabin, into which he could see from where he sat in my cabin – our general messplace. The noise would be such as a drunken person staggering about or falling against things in the cabin, creating a great disturbance; indeed, so much so that it was impossible for him to proceed in his reading; he would therefore step and call out, "Don't make a noise there, steward" (thinking it was the steward rummaging about) and on the noise ceasing, he would continue his reading until again and again interrupted in a similar way, when he would, receiving no answer to his question, "What are you doing, steward, making such a damned noise?" get up, take the candle, and go into the cabin, and come back saying, "Well, I suppose it is the ghost, for there is nothing there"; and on again reading, and the same occurring, he would say to me, "Now do you hear that? is there not some person there?" I would answer: "Yes; I am positive there is; it must be someone drunk who has got down into the cabin, wanting, perhaps, to speak to me"; and so convinced was I that I would get up, and with Mr Macfarlane, go into and search the cabin, but to no purpose! All this had happened repeatedly night after night. Sometimes the noise would be such as the opening of drawers or lockers of the seats, moving decanters, tumblers on the racks, or other articles, in fact, as though everything in the cabin was moved or disturbed. All this time the ship was at anchor more than a mile from the shore; and here I must remark that there was no communication whatever with the fore part of the ship and the cabin; access being by the companion ladder directly between the two cabins, the door of each being at the foot of the ladder; and from one cabin you could see distinctly into the other; so that no person could escape from either up the ladder without being seen.

On one occasion, I and the Master (Mr Macfarlane) had been on shore to drink tea at a friend's house, at Queensferry, near Chester, the vessel being lashed to the lower stage opposite Chunah's quay, and on returning about ten o'clock together, just as I was descending the companion ladder, I distinctly (as I thought) heard some person rush from the after cabin into the fore cabin, it being quite dark at the time. I therefore stopped Mr Macfarlane, who was behind me at the top of the ladder, and whispered to him, "Stand still, a moment, I think I have caught the ghost", and then descended into my cabin, took down my sword from over the bed where it always hung, placed it drawn in his hand, and said, "Now Macfarlane, allow no one to pass you; if anyone attempts to escape, cut him down; I will stand the consequences." I then returned to the cabin, struck a light, and searched everywhere, but nothing could I find, or to account for what I had heard: but I will say, truly, I never felt more certain of anything in my life than I did of finding a man there! and I had to repeat the old saying so often repeated between us, "Oh, it's only the ghost again!" I have often, when lying in bed at night, heard noises as though my drawers were being opened and shut, the top of the washing stand raised and shut down carelessly, the jallousies of the opposite bed places opened and shut, etc; and of an evening, when sitting in my cabin, I have often heard as it were a percussion cap snap close to the back of my head. I have also very, very often (and I say it with reverence and godly fear) been sensible of the presence of something invisible about me, and could have put my hand as it were on it, or the spot where it was, so convinced was I; and all this occurred without me feeling the least alarmed, or caring a bit about it, more than that I could not understand it, or account for what I felt or heard.

On one occasion, the ship being at anchor in Mostyn Roads, I was awoke by the quarter-master coming to call me, and asking me to come on deck, for that the lookout man had rushed down on the lower deck, saying that there was the figure of a female standing on the paddle-box pointing with her finger up to heaven. I felt angry and told him to send the lookout man up on deck again, and keep him there til daylight; but on attempting to carry my orders in to execution the man went into violent convulsions, and the result was I had to get on deck myself and attend to him, and remain till day broke, but nothing was seen by me.

This apparition was often seen afterwards, and as precisely as first described pointing upwards with her finger, and strangely enough as she was last seen by an utter stranger to the whole affair she disappeared, as will be hereafter described.

On another occasion, when lying in the Haverfordwest River, opposite to Lawrenny, on a Sunday afternoon – the crew all being on shore, except my steward and two hands who pulled me on shore to church - during my absence the steward was going down into my cabin when he was spoken to by an unseen voice and fell down instantly with fright, and I found his appearance so altered in my coming on board that I hardly knew him, and extracted the above tale from him, at the same time begging to be allowed his discharge, and to be landed as soon as possible, to which I felt obliged to consent as he could not be persuaded to remain on-board through the night. The story of the ship being haunted seemed to get known on shore, and the clergyman of Lawrenny (Mr Phillips) called on me one day and begged to be allowed to question the crew, which he accordingly did and seemed to view the matter in a serious light and expressed his belief that there was a troubled spirit lingering on board the ship wanting to make known the murder of a beautiful girl, which occurred when the vessel was carrying passengers, and which was as follows:-

The Asp had been engaged as a mail packet between Port Patrick in Scotland and Donaghadee, Ireland, and on running one of her trips, and the passengers supposed to have landed, the stewardess went down into the ladies' cabin where, to her surprise and horror, there lay a beautiful young woman, with her throat cut, in one of the sleeping berths, quite dead, but how she came by her death none could tell, and it was never known. Of course the circumstance gave rise to much mystery and talk, and the vessel was at once removed from the station by the authorities, the matter hushed up, and she had been laid aside and never been used again till handed over to us for surveying service.

During the successive years that I commanded the Asp I lost several of my men, some of whom ran on being refused their discharge, and others I felt I must let go, who declared that they saw a transparent figure of a female at night (all giving the same account) pointing with the finger up to the skies. I had for a year endeavoured to ridicule the whole affair, and each account as often told me (for I was often put to inconvenience in my duties by the loss of hands); indeed, I believe neither steward nor boy would have gone down into the cabin after dark when the officers were out of the ship if you had paid them for it. I myself was awoke one night by a hand (to all sensation) being placed on my leg outside the bedclothes. I laid still for a moment to satisfy myself that such was the case, and then grabbed at it and pulled my bell, which was immediately over my head, for the quarter-master to come down with his lantern, but there was nothing. This has occurred to me several times and precisely as related; but on another occasion a hand was distinctly placed on my forehead, and I believe if ever man's hair stood on end mine did at that moment, and I sprang out of bed – but there was no sound, nothing! Until then I had never felt the least fear or care about the ghost, or whatever it could be, but on the contrary it had been a sort of amusement to me in the night time as I lay in bed to listen to the unaccountable noises in my cabin, and when I felt there was some person there (probably playing tricks) to suddenly pull my bell for the look-out man, and listen most attentively if I could hear the least sound of a footstep or attempt to escape, but there was none. I could hear the look-out man walk from his post to my cabin door, when I merely asked some questions as to the wind or weather. It may be fancied that there were rats or mice in the ship, but I can confidently declare that there were neither...

At length, the vessel requiring repairs, was ordered alongside the dockyard of Pembroke, and the first night the sentry stationed near the ship declared that he saw a female mount the paddle-box, holding up her hands towards the heavens, and step on shore; she came along the path towards him, when he brought his musket to with the charge, "Who goes there?" She then walked through his musket, which he dropped, and ran to the guard-house. The next sentry describes the same thing, and he immediately fired off his musket to alarm the guard. The third sentry, placed near the ruins of Pater old church, says he saw the same figure, which mounted the top of a grave in the old churchyard and stood pointing up to heaven until she gradually vanished out of sight. The sergeant of the guard came with rank and file to learn the tale of the frightened sentries along the dockyard wall, who would not remain at their posts unless the posts were doubled, which I believe they were, and as may be seen in the report of guards for that night.

Singular enough, since that night the ghost has never been seen or heard on board the Asp, nor sounds or noises as before, and it seems as if the spirit or whatever it was departed from her that night inscrutable to all.

This ends my tale, and much as I know one gets laughed at for telling ghost stories or believing in them, I can only say I have given them with all truth as far as

I know and believe, and you are welcome to make what use you please of the same. With kind regards, yours truly,

G.M. Alldridge.'

Despite the little echo of supernatural fiction here, in the way the letter comes to us from a separate named figure, and a third anonymous one (compare especially Sheridan Le Fanu), this looks on the whole about as sober and authentic as a ghost story could be. Aside from the fact that Alldridge was originally wholly sceptical – if not derisive – about ghosts, this story is something of a test-case as regards hoaxing. As the phrase 'ship-shape' reminds us, naval vessels are obsessively orderly and well-monitored places. Not only that, but in many cases this one must have been entirely inaccessible to intruders, who could scarcely have approached or boarded it when it was well off-shore.

We could certainly file this under poltergeists as easily as we could under apparitions. Notice, for example, how precisely the sound of that 'percussion cap' snapping behind Alldridge's head echoes the sound of the pistol shot at Mytton Old Hall in 1804. And then there is 'the presence of something invisible about me'. This might at first seem rather vague. But given how sceptical Alldridge was when he first heard the rumours of the ship's ghost, it is hard not to be struck by his later, very emphatic assertion, 'and [I] could have put my hand ... on it, or the spot where it was, so convinced was I'. And which of us, after all, has not at some point correctly sensed, just before entering a room, that someone, wholly silent and motionless, was already in there?

The Naval Biographical Dictionary tells us that George Manley Alldridge entered the Navy on 13 July 1829, and held various posts around the world in following decades, being present at the capture of 144 pirates off the island of Thasos some time before he took charge of the Asp.

79. The Devils' Camera?

Morning Post, 15 September 1870.
'The Latest American Wonder'.

'The city of St Lawrence, Massachusetts, has been thrown into a state of greatest excitement, and not without just cause. It seems from the account given in the *New York Herald* that an elderly lady lately died in a house on Broadway, in that place. On 20th August, the day after the funeral, a lady who happened to be visiting one of the tenants of the same house accidentally turned her eyes upwards, and distinctly saw the figure of the deceased lady at the attic window. In great consternation she communicated the circumstance to the other occupants of the building, and in a short time the entire neighbourhood were made acquainted with the interesting fact, and with their own eyes witnessed the phenomenon. Various means were tried to expunge the photograph of the ghost, but all in vain; and, at last, owing to the crowds that assembled it was found necessary to remove the sash. Dr William D. Lamb, an eminent physician, subsequently obtained permission to remove the sash to his office in Essex Street, where it has been examined by intelligent and scientific men - some of whom are of opinion that the departed must have been photographed upon the window-pane by the action of lightning when sitting in the room before her death. It is a most uncomfortable story, and it is to be hoped that the intelligent and scientific men will not leave the window sash alone until they have thoroughly sifted the mystery.'

Surely, if His Satanic Majesty was going to take a picture, he would use lightning? This turns out to be a surprisingly tricky question... Of the three physicists I consulted on this, two were very doubtful that lightning could act on window glass in this way. A third, however, referred me to Chidambaram Ramesh's book, *Lightning as a "Photographer"*. Here there can be found a number of similar cases, as well as stories of how people or animals struck by lightning have had the images of leaves or trees printed on their skin. Other victims who survived lightning strikes display fractal patterns effectively tattooed onto their bodies.

One particularly famous incident of alleged lightning photography was supposed to have occurred in 1876, at the Pickens County Courthouse in Carrollton, Alabama. A freed slave called Henry Wells was being held at the top of the building, on suspicion of an arson attack which had burned down the previous Courthouse. With a lynch mob gathered outside and Wells fearing for his life, lightning struck. Although Wells' fate remains uncertain, he does indeed seem to have been killed by the mob. What is now more definitely known is that, the next day, a passerby saw at an upper window a curious image on the glass. This, believed to be the 'lightning photograph' of Wells' terrified face, can still be seen today. Like the St Lawrence image, the Carrollton one resisted all attempts to clean it off. Given that these two cases fell within six years of each other, it is worth wondering about the particular chemical properties of older glass, as opposed to more modern windowpanes. Devilish or not, there seem enough instances of lightning photography to perhaps classify it as 'supernatural' in the sense used by the scientist Lyall Watson, whose classic work, *Supernature*, explores the uncertain boundaries between known science and seemingly fantastical aspects of the natural world.[7]

80. The Ghostly Vicar.

Royal Cornwall Gazette, 23 March 1893.

'A ghost has had the temerity to invade the house of the Rev. G.S. Tyler, a Wesleyan minister at 27, St George's Road, Kilburn ... The house has, for many years now, been the dwelling place of the various ministers who have succeeded each other every three years at the Quex Road chapel. Mr Tyler and his family have lived there now for 18 months. "I have never seen the apparition myself," said Mr Tyler, "and have always been a confirmed unbeliever in spirit manifestations, and so on. But the fact remains, explain it how you will, that my wife and my daughters Ada and Julie, aged respectively 20 and 19 years, have distinctly seen a mysterious something, which, in the absence of any better way of describing it, we have called an apparition. They agree closely in their several descriptions of the figure. It is that of a person attired as a Wesleyan minister might be, in black clothes of a clerical cut. It is a figure of average stature, with a long grey beard, and keen peculiar eyes. It was my younger daughter who first met with the apparition. She will tell you in her own way."

Miss Julie Tyler then took up the story. "I was standing at the corner of the stairs", she said, "and I saw what I took to be pa. I had gone to call him to tea, and when I called him he neither answered nor moved. I thought that he was playing with me, and giving me the trouble to go up to him, and I ran up to push him. I pushed right through the figure and fell against the wall. I was dreadfully frightened, but when I told the others they laughed at me. But then Ada, later on, saw the same figure, and then mother herself. It was before Christmas that I saw it. No, I had not been reading any ghost stories at all then. But I have since. So have we all."

Miss Ada then related her experience of the uncanny visitor. She was alone in the house with a child one Sunday evening, and saw the figure in the doorway. She thought a man had broken into the house at first, until she observed the clerical cut of the figure's garb, and then recalled her sister's experience. Mrs Tyler's statement was that, while passing by the small room at the end of the passage one evening, she saw Mr Tyler standing in there, as she thought. She ran upstairs to the study, and there found the actual Mr Tyler in the flesh. It is in this room at the end of the passage, indeed, where this apparition has been most frequently seen, and the ladies of the household do not care to venture near it alone. It is a small room looking out onto the back garden, but with wooden shutters, which are fastened over the glass in the evening. "It was in that room" said Miss Julie, "that I met the figure face to face. I shall never forget his eyes – greyish blue in colour, and they seemed to look through me quite hungrily".

It was a strange experience, a Pall Mall reporter says, to sit listening to these ghost stories, in broad daylight, for the minister and his wife were responsible, unemotional, clear-headed folk, and the two girls are bright, intelligent, English girls, with an absence of any indications of hysterical dispositions. They were as firmly convinced that they had seen some unaccountable figure as that they had seen the streets of Kilburn when they looked out of the window. The minister, while expressing utter inability to account for the declarations of his family, would not commit himself to any belief in the supernatural, but betrayed an interest in the whole subject which did not dovetail into his strained attempts to laugh the matter over. In reply to further questions he said that one of the Wesleyan ministers who had preceded him had died in this house; and that when he told his friends of his family's experiences, he discovered for the first time that Mrs Gibson, the wife of his immediate predecessor in the house, had also met with some uncanny experiences. Asked whether he had taken certain floors up in his hunt for some explanation of the mystery – for so ran the gossip of the neighbourhood – the reverend gentleman said that in the top bedroom there had long been a recurrent and intermittent smell of an utterly indescribable kind. The room was quite away from drains or anything which he could imagine as the cause for the effluvium, and the floor had been taken up in the search for the origin of the nuisance. Perhaps in the same manner that Mr Stead's "Julia" writes his copy, this mysterious clerical spirit comes to assist Mr Tyler in the preparation of his sermons.'

These closing lines refer to William Thomas Stead, who claimed to communicate with a dead American journalist, Julia Ames, during the 1890s. Despite that rather weak joke, the reporter here looks fairly open-minded on the whole. They had some reason to be. Notice that none of the three women seem to have been inclined to see ghosts. Both daughters at first thought they were looking at an ordinary person – a very common perception amongst people who have seen ghosts. Moreover, after Julia's first sighting, her mother and her sister briskly laugh the matter off until they see the spectre. Notice, too, that Mrs Gibson, the last tenant, had kept quiet about her startling experiences in the house until she was prompted. This is utterly typical of the way people handle their own personal ghost or poltergeist stories. If you nudge them, you may find out; but if you do not, you can know the person intimately for years and never hear a thing.

Apart from the rather ironic claim of the minister that he 'would not commit himself to any belief in the supernatural' (God? angels? devils? heaven? hell?), another interesting detail here is the smell. This is mentioned in the

Cambridge apparition case, and is a pretty common feature of poltergeist incidents – sometimes being pleasant, sometimes foul. In two cases personally related to me, there was a smell of pipe smoke and of burned toast.

The way that Julia falls right through the ghost on first sighting is also memorable. It might seem pretty obvious that ghosts should not be solid; but it is perhaps worth citing a fairly recent instance of this, given our tendency to take recent evidence more seriously than the tales of a century past. The Langham Hilton Hotel in London has had an impressive number of ghost sightings or experiences (including ones from England cricketers in June 2014), but it is hard to beat that reported by the veteran BBC broadcaster James Alexander Gordon.

In 1973 the hotel building was owned by the BBC, which used it for staff on very late or early shifts. After his first ever midnight news broadcast Gordon went to bed relieved after a successful debut, only to wake and find himself looking at a fluorescent ball of light across the room. This presently transformed into a man dressed in Victorian evening wear. When Gordon demanded what the man wanted, the ghost began to float towards him. It had piercing eyes, and was about two feet off the ground. Gordon seized one of his boots, and hurled it at the apparition – only to have it pass straight through. Interestingly, Gordon notes at one point in his story that, though he could see through the spectre, he had to try hard to do so: at a glance it looked pretty much solid. Typically enough, it was only when Gordon told his story to other BBC staff that they readily confessed to having seen the ghost as well.

The Evil Eye

Your friends have just had a baby, and invite you round to see the child for the first time. Standard protocol for such an occasion is, of course, well known: 'Oh! isn't s/he beautiful? Can I have him/her?' For most of history, however, this was exactly the *wrong* thing to do when confronted with someone else's lovely new infant. Why? Because it meant you were *envious* of the lovely baby, and therefore you had very probably cast the evil eye upon it, and made it sick. Accordingly, the right thing to do for most of history was to say, 'Oh! what a lovely baby!' and then spit on the floor – this being a magical way of undoing any envious spell you might have cast, intentionally or otherwise. Anyone who finds this unhygienic could try the alternative version, which was to coo, 'Oh! what a lovely baby!', followed by, 'but not really!' – this latter being a formula designed, again, to undo any potential curse.

The word 'envy' is itself related to the Latin *invidere*, 'to look maliciously upon'; whilst in India today, babies have a spot painted on their foreheads as protection against the jealousy of infertile women, who may cast the evil eye upon them. But envy does not seem to have been the only reason why a person gained the dubious reputation of having such power. One other reason seems to have been the ordinary bad luck of being afflicted with a squint, or something else which made your eye or eyes look different (note, again, the magical attitude to disability). This applies in part to the wonderful tale of the Chick family and their sinister cat. Other people who gained the reputation seem to have been those who were generally considered unlucky or accident prone. A disproportionate number of bad things were thought to happen around them, and while they were not personally blamed for intending this, the evil eye was often used to explain the perception of their Jonah-like qualities.

One other category was people whose eyes were, simply, powerful. This may well explain why Byron was thought by some to have the evil eye (what, after all, did he have to be envious of?). And it also probably explains, in part, one of the oldest cases on record. In the New Testament Acts of the Apostles, we hear of how, on the island of Cyprus, St Paul and his Christian mafia muscle in on the existing spiritual operation and convince the governor, Paulus, that they are able to offer better protection than the current magician, one Bar-jesus. With this 'false prophet' still resisting the interlopers, Paul, being 'filled with the Holy Ghost, set his eyes on him, And said, O full of all subtlety and all mischief, [thou] child of the devil, [thou] enemy of all righteousness, wilt thou not cease to pervert the right ways of the Lord? And now, behold, the hand of the Lord [is] upon thee, and thou shalt be blind, not seeing the sun for a season. And immediately there fell on him a mist and a darkness; and he went about seeking some to lead him by the hand' (Acts, 13.9-11).

This story is almost certainly true. But what actually happened? First: if anyone in the New Testament was going to have a powerful stare, it would undoubtedly be the egotistical and ferociously zealous St Paul, a man with all the unbalanced fervour of the recent convert (not long since, Paul had been helpfully holding people's coats while they stoned St Stephen to death). Second: Bar-jesus himself almost certainly believed in the power of the evil eye. Accordingly, in a less extreme version of all those cases of voodoo death, Bar-jesus' own fear made him blind – or rather, made him temporarily blind. This is a known medical phenomenon, sometimes referred to as conversion disorder, and widely recorded not only in magical cultures, but in cases of shell-shock, where soldiers could be struck temporarily mute without obvious physiological cause. Why do Christians seem so reluctant to talk about this episode? Aside from the fact of Paul's behaviour looking, as it were, rather 'unChristian', there is another interesting reason. It is almost certain that some of the blind people cured by Christ were not born blind, but – like Bar-jesus – merely suffering from temporary, psychosomatic blindness. Belief had made them sick, and faith of a kind made them well.

I trust everyone now knows what to do next time they see a lovely new baby.

81. Given the Eye.
The Hull Packet, 2 December 1836.

'Last week a married woman of the name of Oates, residing at Mould Green, near Huddersfield, attempted to put a period to her existence, by cutting her throat, and but slight hopes are entertained of her recovery. She gives the following singular reason as the cause of the rash act. Some months ago a travelling writing master knocked at the door, which she opened, and he eyed her over in such a manner, that she could not get it off her mind, and she became firmly persuaded that he had *bewitched* her. She states that she had frequently made the matter a subject of fervent prayer, but could not do away with the delusion.'

82. 'Witch-Burning in Russia'.
The Standard, 11 November 1879.
From our own correspondent in Berlin, 7 Nov.

'Agrafena Ignatjewa was as a child simple and amiable, neither sharper nor more stupid than all the other girls of her native village, Wratschewo, in the government of

Novgorod. But the people of the place having, from their early youth, made up their minds that she had the "evil eye", nothing could eradicate that impression.

Being branded with this reputation it naturally followed that powers of divination and enchantment were attributed to her, including the ability to affect both men and animals with various plagues and sicknesses.

In spite, however, of the supernatural skill with which she was credited, she met with no suitor save a poor soldier. She accepted him gladly, and going with him, shortly after her marriage, to St Petersburg, Wratschewo lost sight of her for some twelve years. She was, however, by no means forgotten there, for when, after the death of her husband, she again betook herself to the home of her childhood, she found that her old reputation still clung to her. The news of her return spread like wildfire, and general disaster was anticipated from her injurious spells. This, however, was, from fear, talked of only behind her back, and dread of her at length reached such a pitch that the villagers and their wives sent her presents and assisted her in every way, hoping thereby to get into her good graces, and so escape being practised upon by her infernal arts. As she was now fifty years of age, somewhat weakly, and therefore unable to earn a living, these attentions were by no means unwelcome, and she therefore did nothing to disabuse her neighhbours' minds. Their superstition enabled her to live comfortably and without care, and she knew very well that any assurances she might give would not have produced the slightest effect.

A short time after her return to Wratschewo, several women fell ill. This was, of course, laid at the door of Ignatjewa, particularly as one of these women, the daughter of a peasant, had been attacked [with sickness] immediately after being refused a slight favour by her*. Whenever any misfortune whatsoever happened in the village, all fingers pointed to Ignatjewa as the source of it. At the beginning of the present year a dismissed soldier, in the interest of the community, actually instituted criminal proceedings against her before the local *urjadnik*, the chief of the police of the district, the immediate charge preferred being that she had bewitched his wife.

Meanwhile the feeling in the villlage against her became so intensified that it was resolved by the people, pending the decision on the complaint that had been lodged, to take the law into their hands so far as to fasten her up in her cottage.

The execution of this resolve was not delayed a moment. Led by Kauschin, Nikisorow, Starovij, and an old man of seventy, named Schipensk, whose wife and daughters were at the time supposed to be suffering from her witchcraft, a crowd of villagers set out on the way to Ignatjewa's dwelling. Nikisorow had provided

259

himself with hammer and nails, and Iwanow with some chips of pinewood "to smoke out the bad spirits". Finding the cottage door locked, they beat it in, and while a portion of them nailed up the windows, the remainder crowded in and announced to the terrified woman that, by unanimous decision, she was, for the present, to be kept fastened up in her house. Some of them proceeded to look through the rooms, where they found, unfortunately, several bottles containing medicaments. Believing these to be enchanted potions, and therefore conclusive proofs of Ignatjewa's guilt, it was decided, on the suggestion of Nikisorow, to burn her and her devilish work there and then. "We must put an end to it," shouted the peasants in chorus, "if we let her off now we shall be bewitched one and all."

Kauschin, who held in his hand a lighted chip of pinewood, which he had used to "smoke out the spirits" and to light him about the premises, instantly applied it to a bundle of straw lying in a room, after which all hastily left. Ignatjewa attempted in vain to follow them. The agonised woman then tried to get out at the windows, but these were already nailed up. In front of the cottage stood the people, blankly staring at the spreading flames, and listening to the cries of their victim without moving a muscle.

At this point Ignatjewa's brother came on the scene, and ran towards the cottage to rescue his sister. But a dozen arms held him back. "Don't let her out", shouted the venerable Schipensk, the husband and father of the bewitched women, "I'll answer for it." "That we won't, father; we have put up with her long enough", replied one of the band. "The Lord be praised!", exclaimed another, "let her burn away; she bewitched my daughters too."

The little room in which Ignatjewa had taken refuge was not as yet reached by the fire. Appeals were now made to her to confess herself a witch, the brother joining, probably in the hope that if she did so her life might be spared. "But I am entirely innocent," the poor woman cried out. One of the bystanders, apparently the only one in possession of his five senses, made another attempt at rescue, but was hindered by the mob. He then, in loud tones, warned them of the punishment which would certainly await them, but in vain, no attention was paid to him. On the contrary, the progress of the flames not appearing rapid enough, it was endeavoured to accelerate it by shoving the snow from the roof and loosening the framework. The fire now extended rapidly, one beam after another blazed up, and at length the roof fell in on the wretched woman.

The ashes smouldered the whole night; on the following morning nothing was found remaining but the charred bones of Ignatjewa.

The idea now, it would seem, occurred to the murderers that perhaps, after all, their action had not

261

been altogether lawful. They accordingly resolved to bribe the local authority, who had already viewed the scene of the affair, to hush it up. For this purpose they made a collection, and handed him the proceeds, 21 roubles 90 copecks. To their astonishment, he did not accept the money, but at once reported the horrible deed to his superior officer. Sixteen of the villagers were, in consequence, brought up for trial at Tichwin before the district court Novgorod, on the charge of murdering Agrafena Ignatjewa, in the manner above described.

After a protracted hearing with jury, the following result was arrived at: Kauschin, who had first set fire to the building; Starovij, who had assisted in accelerating the burning; and Nikisorow, the prime mover in the matter, who had nailed up the windows, were found guilty, and sentenced by the judge to some slight ecclesiastical penance, while the remaining thirteen, including the aged Schipensk – who had used his influence to prevent a rescue – went scot free.'

*This is probably another classic case of psychosomatic illness, or conversion disorder: just as Bar-jesus and Emma Smith had done, the woman makes herself ill because she expects harm from Ignatjewa. Unless phrasing is incorrect, the above example is unusual insofar as most cases involved the 'witch' being refused a favour, not the victim.

262

One little part of this tragic tale is particularly interesting: so far as we know, Agrafena never had any such troubles (or benefits) during her twelve-odd years in Petersburg. Perhaps people here were less superstitious; but the London tale of 1885 (just below) shows us that city-folk could be as magically-inclined as country-dwellers. Perhaps, in fact, Agrafena's reputation at Wratschewo was not based on what her eyes *looked like*; hence no one noticing her in Petersburg, which in turn suggests that the evil eye was not always a matter of appearance. There is, however, a hint that her powers were exercised through her eyes: did the peasants first shut her up in the cottage so that she could not *look* at any of them?

83. Extraordinary Murder.
The Dundee Courier, 26 December 1884.

'An extraordinary murder has just been committed at St Romain Les Atheux, in the Loire departement. The victim, a farmer named Ravel, was attacked at 9 o'clock pm about thirty yards from his house, and his corpse was found soon afterwards, pierced with wounds and covered with stones. Ravel was a powerfully-built man, and the ground round was torn up, showing signs of a severe struggle, in which several assailants must have taken part. He was credited in the country with having the evil eye, and was believed by many of his neighbours to have brought about the death of their cattle. The magistrates, after investigating the case, have arrived at the conviction that the murder of Ravel is to be traced entirely to this cause'.

84. A Shaggy Cat Story.
The North-Eastern Daily Gazette, 26 December 1885.

Confronted with the following extraordinary tale, part of me thinks: we only have this staggering glimpse into the popular mind because a) Kadgewick assaulted Chick, and b) because the resourceful journalist decided to pursue Chick and interview him. Another part of me thinks there's perhaps a 10% chance that the journalist made some of it up. But if they did, don't you wish they'd become a novelist?

Bear with it til the end, and I'll attempt a coherent summary. It may help in advance to know that the chief players are: Kadgewick, who commits the assault; Mr Chick, his victim; and four generations of women: Chick's wife, her mother, and her grandmother, along with the grandmother's aunt.

'Jeremiah Kadgewick, a costermonger, was charged before the magistrate with committing a violent and unprovoked assault on John Chick, by striking him on the head with an iron rod, used to support a paraffin-lamp at his fish-stall. The prosecutor, who appeared with a strip of sticking plaster across his forehead, said he kept a fruit and vegetable stall a short distance from the one used by the prisoner, and that on the previous evening, shortly before ten o'clock, having packed up his things on a barrow, he was passing Kadgewick on his way home, when the latter made a blow at him with the iron rod, at the same time alluding to his (prosecutor's) wife, and using an opprobrious epithet concerning her, and remarking that the "whack" wasn't intended so much for him as for her, and that she deserved it ten times hotter than that.

Witnesses having been called to corroborate prisoner's statement, the magistrate commented on the savage and unmanly nature of the assault, and inquired of the prisoner what he had to say. Kadgewick replied that as far as the unmanliness of it went, he thought that the boot was on the other leg. It was the prosecutor who was unmanly in not taking steps to prevent his wife being the terror of all who had the misfortune to offend her. "If I had been unmanly, your worship", said Kadgewick, who seemed much hurt at the insinuation, "I should ha' pitched into her instead of him." "But how do you justify your visiting the sins of the wife on the husband?" "Your worship", responded Jeremiah Kadgewick in impressive tones, "when a man is drove off his head with wildness he can't weigh and medjur whys and wherefores like he can at another time. It is all owing to Jack Chick's wife having a "evil eye"'.

There was considerable laughter in court at this, but prisoner maintained a grave demeanour, and nodded his head in the manner of a man quite confident of presently being able to prove his position. When order was restored he proceeded, "I hain't the only one that knows it, and has suffered by it. ("Not by a good many, Jerry", in a female voice from someone in court, with several 'Hear, hears'.) There's others besides me who has suffered from her spitefulness, and it is time it was stopped. She can put a crab, your worship, on a man's luck, or on a man's goods at any time she chooses by giving one of her meaning looks at them. That's how she served me yesterday evening. I'd got as nice a lot of mackerel as ever was sold and was laying 'em out on the stall when she came across and asked me in a ordering sort of way to take a ticket for a benefit raffle for her father-in-law. I said I had other means for my money without wasting it on those who was always getting drunk and being run in by the police, when she answers, 'Very well, you will find then that you can less afford to say "no" than "yes"', and then she 'screws a squint' at my fish and walks off. And, believe me, or believe me not, your worship", continued Mr Kadgewick, growing warmer, but so help me it is true, I never sold another blessed mackerel for near an hour, and at last when a customer came to the stall she smelt at 'em, and I knew by her way of shaking her head as she walked away what she meant. She was right, too. They had gone wrong! Fresh and bright as new buttons, your worship, before tea time, and gone wrong before eight o'clock. Wot do you think of her? If you don't believe me, there she is in court – have her for'ad and let her deny it if she can."

As the prisoner uttered these last words he pointed excitedly to a buxom-looking young woman, smartly dressed, and wearing a hat with an ostrich feather, and on the prosecutor acknowledging her to be his wife, the magistrate desired her to get into the witness box. She was by no means an unpleasant looking female, and on being questioned she gave a flat denial to all that Kadgewick had sworn to as to her putting a spell on his mackerel with her "evil eye". "Have you an 'evil eye'?" his worship smilingly enquired. "Do I look as though I had, sir?" said she, with an artless glance towards the bench. "It is nothing but a monstrous and ridiculous excuse on the prisoner's part", the magistrate remarked, "and he must pay twenty shillings or go to prison for fourteen days." No doubt the decision was a righteous one; nevertheless the woman's eyes were undoubtedly peculiar, and the case being settled and his worship engaged in a whispered conversation with his clerk, quick as lightning Mrs Chick 'screwed a squint' at Jeremiah Kadgewick, the effect of which was to make him change colour and to elicit mutterings of indignation from his friends and sympathisers. The fine was paid, however, and feeling inquisitive to learn ... to what extent Mr Chick believed in his partner's evil eye, I left the court when he did, and contrived shortly afterwards an opprtunity for some conversation with him.'

(The reporter now admits that he was the more curious because he had recently seen a court case where a woman was accused of fortune telling, and hired a barrister, whose services must have cost several pounds. He was surprised to find that the husband had provided the necessary funds, though the two were separated, and there was a strong animosity between them. When the woman was sentenced to four months' hard labour, the husband remarked, "Serve her well right; I wish it was as many years." On questioning the husband about the oddity of this, the reporter was told, "That woman, sir, if she liked, could bewitch me to that extent my life would be a misery to me.")

'With this incident fresh in my memory I was the less surprised to find Mr Chick a steadfast believer in his wife's "evil eye". He looked anything but the sort of man to be influenced by foolish superstition, and was indeed exceptionally wide-awake and shrewd-looking even for his class. He was several years older than his wife, and apparently in easy circumstances. Was there any foundation, I asked him, for what the fish-stall keeper had stated. To which Mr Chick replied dubiously, and as though, up to this time, he had been unable to make up his mind whether it was a matter to deplore or be proud of, "There's that amount of foundations for it, sir, that I could, in a manner of speaking, show you whole rows of hinstances built on 'em." "Can it be in any way accounted for?" "Well, if it comes to that," he replied after a pause, and slowly puffing at his pipe, "it's well-known how she came by it. Leastways, when I say well-known, it ain't no secret in the family. She got it off her grandmother." "How do you mean got it off her? Am I to understand that the 'evil eye', as it is called, is hereditary with your wife's people?". "Oh dear no," returned Mr Chick, gravely shaking his head, "there's more in it than readitairy – it's ackshal fact, and not got out of books. Anyhow, the family believe it, and d'ye see, it's more likely to be true since it isn't anything to brag about. It is said to have been 'anded down to her from her grandmother in this way.

When she – the grandmother, I mean – was a youngish woman, she was parted from her husband, very likely because he couldn't put up with her tricks any longer, and she lived along with an aunt who seems to have been a queer sort of old stick herself. I don't know how she got hold of it, but she had a lot of money, and she lived in a big old house which used to be pinted out to me, close to the Surrey Sulogical gardens before it was built on. The aunt she didn't keep any servant, cept the party we're speaking of. She used to do the work, and sit along of the old woman to keep her company when she'd done it.

Well, though the niece knowed her aunt had got money, she never could find out where she kept it. She had a lot of small house property and she used to go round, Monday mornings, to get the rents; but what became of 'em when she'd got 'em was a blessed mystery to the niece. She didn't put it in the bank, and she didn't spend it in wittles and drink, that was certain – being a rare old skin-flint in that line. She'd bring it home – the money, I mean – five and six pounds, and always in silver, and count it out on the table, as lief before the other as not, and then she'd pop it in the bag, and that was the last that was seen of it. It wasn't for want of hunting after it that the niece didn't find out where it was stowed, but, though she kept the sharpest of eyes on the old lady, and searched in every likely corner, it was all no good. The money vanished, somehow or other.

But one night, a couple of hours after [the niece] had been abed – she slept atop of the house, and the other on the first floor, she heard the creaking of a opening door, and nipping out onto the landing to see what it was, she looked over the banisters, and then she spies a figure in white gliding down the stairs. Most women would have been frightened, but she wasn't wanting in pluck, and she made out at once that it was the old woman in her bedgown. Slipping a black frock over her own bedgown, so as not to be conspickyus, she went soft with her naked feet downstairs, too – right down to the basement, where there was a sort of cellar, that was damp, and ratty, and pitch dark, the iron grating that used to let the light in being boarded up, and as far as the niece knowed it was never used for anything. Well, without any candle or lamp, the old woman she unlocks the cellar door, and goes in, shutting it after her, and the niece listening at the keyhole hears a chinking sound, that meant nothing but money. All in the pitch dark she stayed there so long that her niece got cramp in her legs standing on the stone steps, and then hearing her coming out, she sloped upstairs quick, and again looking over the banisters, saw her aunt come up and go back into her bedroom.

So, very next day, the niece she sets about overhauling the cellar. I ain't going to say anything about her motives, it being no affair of mine. It might ha' been only female curiosity, or it might ha' been that she meant helping herself if she found that there was so much money that a little wouldn't be missed. Anyway, she found another key that would fit the lock, and before the old woman was up, she got into the cellar with a candle to see with. But she had her trouble for nothing. There was nothing there barring a old cupboard, and that was quite empty, and as she could see by the rust on the firegrate and the thick soot the hiding-place was not up the chimney. There was not a single article of furniture or any lumber that money could be stowed among, and after hunting ever so long she had to give it up. But the idea had got into her head, and it sort of haunted her. She waited till the night of the next Monday, when the old woman had collected her rents, and sure enough she sees her creeping down and visiting the cellar like she did the week before, and she listened, and again she heard the chinking.

"As for what follers after that," continued Mr Chick, refreshing himself, "you can please yourself about believing it. I've heard it lots of times from one and the other of my wife's relatives, and I've heard it from her as well, but pon my sivey [slang for: 'upon my word'], I couldn't tell you for certain what she thinks about it. She's rum that way. 'Now look here, Suke', I've said to her, 'do it stand to sense or reason that it could be so?' But, stead of answering me in words, she laughs, and fixing her eye on mine begins to screw a squint at me, which sends me off, and so there's no more said about it. But, as I was saying, when this niece – my missus's grandmother, you understand – finds out that she can't get at the old lady's hidden money by fair means, she turns her attention to being able to do so by foul. What she wants is to be able to see in the dark, like the cats do. I'll tell you why presently. Well, whether she went to a witch, or what she did, lor' a mighty knows, but she must have done something, for one night as she was laying awake – she may have just been giving the finishing touches to some charm or other, for all I know – she suddenly finds out that she can see in the dark. She could make out the picters on the wall, and what time it was by her watch, which was hanging over the mantel-shelf t'other side of the room. Sunday night this was, so next night – Monday – she puts on her black frock, and when she had bid the old woman good night, 'stead of going up to bed, she slips down to the cellar, and opens the door with her own key, and all in the pitch dark, she goes in and locks it after her, and crouches down in a corner.

There wasn't any mistake about her having the power she wanted. Dark as it was, she could see about the cellar in every corner, whichever way she turned her eyes, so that when, bimeby, she heard her aunt creeping down and opening the door she shut her eyes, and peeped only just out of the corners of 'em, lest she might be bowled out by their shining. The old lady come without any light, as usual, and the other, keeping stiller than a mouse and watching her, saw her make straight for one particular little square stone in the floor against the wall, and which she forced up with a knife. Then she heard her pour the silver money out of her rent-collecting bag into the hole, and after amusing herself with stirring of it all up with both her hands for a little while she put the stone back in its place and went off, locking the cellar door after her, you may be sure. But," continued Mr Chick, "the most singular part of it was wot happened a few days afterward." "I think I can guess," I remarked; "the hoard of money disappeared from the hiding place." "That's wot I should have reckoned on," he answered, with a slow wink, "but it was something more singular even than that. Four mornings afterwards, I think it was, as the story goes, the old aunt is found dead in her bed, and, as she left no will nor no instructions nor nothing it was lucky that the niece knowed where to drop on all her savings." "It is to be hoped," I remarked, that the 'evil eye' had nothing to do with the old lady's sudden going off." Mr Chick made no verbal response for some seconds, but acknowledged my observation by slowly winking with his other eye. Then he said, thoughtfully, "I should hope not. Otherwise it might be orkard for me. I don't think it could have been; as, from all that I've been told about it, them that has a 'evil eye' can't do any harm to them that they are close related to, and this, don't you see, was her aunt."

"But you have not yet told me in what way this wonderful power of vision was handed down, as you say, from the grandmother to the grandchild – to your wife." "Well, no, I didn't tell you about that," replied Mr Chick, with a short laugh, "because it don't seem perlite to offer any one else something to swaller that don't go down easy with yer own self. This ere story of the grey cat don't go down easy with me." "What about a grey cat?". "Well, you must know that accordin' to the yarn they'd have you believe that as soon as my wife's grandmother come into her property a big grey cat that only had one eye come and quartered itself on her, and wouldn't be got rid of. Nobody knowed for certain where it came from, but there seems to be only one opinion about it, and that is, that when the bargain was made about the power to see in the dark, them that it was made with thought it might be as well to have the party wot got the benefit looked after, to prevent her doing anything to shirk the contract. Anyhow, the grey cat couldn't ever be got rid of. Pisening was tried, but without any effect; and once a couple of bricks was tied to its neck, and it was chucked into the canal. But it no more minded them than if they'd been a couple of bungs, and after swimming across it landed and come indoors quite dry and comfortable next morning when the milk was fetched in. Another time – mind jer I'm only telling you what's been told me – the grey cat was hung by the neck and left hanging all night for dead, and next morning it was buried more'n a foot deep, and its missus thought she had got rid of it now for certain.

But she hadn't been long abed before there come a scratching at the door, which she opened, and in walks the grey cat quite friendly, and purring against her legs as though nothing had happened; after which trying to destroy it was given up as a bad job. Old age itself didn't seem able to kill it, for as I've told you it was grey when it made its appearance, and it was still alive thirteen years afterwards when its missus – my wife's grandmother – died. By that time her only daughter – my wife's mother – had growed to be a woman, and was married and had had a young un – my wife as is at present.

And now we're a getting round to how my missus is said to have got her pecooliar powers of wision from her grandmother. How much money there was found in the stone under the cellar was never known to anybody but herself, but the old woman made it fly, and just before she died there wasn't more than a couple of hundred remaining of it. But this she left to her grand-daugher, who she was very fond of, and who then was only a baby a few months old. Very likely she funked about dying, for she begged with her last breath a'most that the child might be brought up straight and proper, and taught to pray for its grandmother. It was said to be noticed that the grey cat, who was in the room at the time, seemed to be took with a sort of fit when it heard these words, and went chasing about with its tail all of a bush, and swearin' orful. But it tamed down a bit when the old woman was gone, and all of a sudden appeared to take uncommon to the baby in its cradle. But the day the old woman was buried it was found in the cradle along with the young un, and sitting on its chest and nosing it about with his whiskers, and the mother finding it so, shrieks out, thinking that the cat was sucking the baby's breath, as the old women say. But when that animal heard the shriek, it leapt out of the cradle and bolted, and was never seen again, and immediately afterwards it was discovered that when the baby got into a passion it began to squint. And now, if you put this and that together", said Mr Chick, bringing his interesting narrative to a conclusion, "you'll be able to make as much out of it as ever I've been able to".

"There is only one thing else I should like to know", I remarked, "and that is, how you came to make up your mind to marry a young woman concerning whom there must have been unpleasant rumours?" "Well", returned Mr Chick, with another of his slow winks, "d'ye see, that these two hundred pounds had been put by for her til she got married, and I weighed it up, and resolved to chance it."

Clearly, we have here many of the elements of a fine ghost or mystery story: hidden treasure; a diabolical pact with a witch or wizard; a dark and sinister familiar in the shape of the indestructible cat; along with strange powers emanating from the eyes, and handed down, somehow, through the generations. Are these gift, or curse? The poor baby, after all, does not seem to have much choice about the bestowal of this power, even if it is artfully manipulated by the adult Mrs Chick in later years. The barest précis of the whole seems to be as follows: the grandmother made some magical bargain, allowing her to see in the dark and locate the treasure; there was no sign of this power in her daughter, but in her granddaughter, Mrs Chick, it resurfaced in altered form as the evil eye. Was the power strictly hereditary? It seems in fact to have been somehow guarded and passed on by the mystery cat, which Chick explicitly identifies as an occult agent, a kind of feline Mephistopheles... who collected, in repayment – what? We have no idea.

Rightly bewildered by this incredible association of seemingly unconnected events, we can cling nonetheless to one solid fact: Mrs Chick had powerful eyes. Indeed, as eyes are as powerful as what lies behind them, she evidently had a powerful presence and personality. Even the educated reporter acknowledges their memorable quality. And so, on that one definite element, the whole wonderful story is assembled, from scraps of family history, almost certainly passed down in purely oral form. It is hard to know whether we should be grateful for this tale having survived, or stricken at the thought of all the similar stories which were lost.

As we have seen, it was by no means just 'old women' who believed that cats sucked the breath of babies.

Religion

As you might by now have come to expect, this is Christianity of a sort, but not as we know it. There again: do we really know what went on in the heads of all those people Christ met in the New Testament? If anything seems to unite most of them, it is indeed their hope that Christ and the apostles could be useful. Beyond that, we are in shadowy territory as to beliefs and motives.

85. The End of the World.
Royal Cornwall Gazette, 7 May 1825.

The *Sherborne Mercury* says, a species of blight or grub has settled on the blackberry leaves, gnawing them in a serpentine manner so that the dead fibre shows through the remaining green. It will hardly be credited by many persons, that in consequence of a certain prophecy, [there] exists a great degree of alarm in the minds of the lower classes residing on the borders of Dorset and Devon. It has gone forth that a "flying serpent" will poison the air, which, becoming impure, will cause the death of nineteen persons out of twenty, and that the time will be known by this particular appearance on the leaves of the blackberry, which the pseudo-prophet calls the reflection of the serpent. Another version of the story has its origin from a a different reading, promulgated by some "wise man" (of whom there are not a few now practising in this and the adjoining counties), that the serpent, whose pestilential influence is to be felt, is none other than Satan, whose period of bondage is now expired. A third account describes, that the deaths will take place principally among persons under thirty years of age. This impudent imposition upon credulity and ignorance gains credit in the nineteenth century, and *hundreds* of individuals have *paid* for charms to secure themselves from danger and infection.'

86. Chase the Devil.
The Times, 22 April 1843.

'This morning (Tuesday) a vast number of the lower classes assembled in a field at the rear of Mr Malcolmson's house. Some of the more respectable classes, who were astir at that time, and passing in the vicinity, very naturally inquired what was the cause of so great an assemblage at such an early hour. The answer given, to their very great surprise, was, "that the Devil was traced all the way from Cashel across to Mr Bank's field, and that the print of his foot was quite visible, the ground being burned." Young and old, halt and lame, were after him, and the chase was kept up with a spirit that completely baffles description. Walls, fences of every kind, and rivers, were taken in the most sporting style to catch "the old boy"; and one of the foremost said "that he had just got a glimpse of him" and that "he was a tall, genteel looking man". On went the chase, and in the meantime intelligence of the pursuit reached the mayor (so much noise did the affair make) and his worship lost no time in summoning Denis F---, who, he conceived, would be a good man in "over-reaching him". Both were quickly mounted, and soon they crossed on the hunt, but the devil was out of sight when they came up with the pursuers, and no trace of him was visible. Hundreds during the day were to be seen going in the direction where the footprints were.'

87. **Frightful Delusion.**
The Belfast-Newsletter, 4 November 1845.

'We have received more than one communication on the subject of an awfully blasphemous mockery now put in practice by more than one priest of the Church of Rome, for the purpose of turning the terrible visitation which has befallen the poor, in the partial failure of the potato crop, into a source of profit, unexampled in its barefaced effrontery, by any delusion that the annals of Popery can furnish. In a brief paragraph in a former number we alluded to a Granard priest, who was said to be selling holy water to the ignorant people, which being sprinkled on the potato, was to avert the calamity, and preserve their sole food from contagion.

We have been favoured with a letter from a highly respectable gentleman, informing us that the Westmeath Guardian, from which we derived our information, was in error in attributing this monstrous outrage against common sense to a Granard priest, as he declares all the Roman Catholic clergymen there are "gentlemen of too much integrity, charity, and high-mindedness to stoop to humour ignorance and superstition", and that it is to another district of the County of Longford the impostor belongs. The price he charges is five shillings to the farmer, and two and sixpence to the cottier, and our correspondent, on whose word we can place the most implicit reliance, assures us that over £700 have already been netted by this novel swindle.

The following is an extract from the communication: "The plan is to bring a quart of salt in a little bag. This is passed by the clerks – for the priest is in such a great way of business, that he is obliged to employ these aids – to the priest, who blesses it. The little bag of salt is then returned to the faithful – for he must be full of faith, and he proves it by giving his money ... The salt is then taken to the field, dissolved in the water, and sprinkled on the ridges, or at least on some of them, as far as it goes. The plague is immediately stopped, and the next day the faithful digs his potatoes, as sound as may be.

It is but justice to the priest and his coadjutor of the parish in which the wizard spreads forth his wand, that they have used all exertions in their power to counteract its operations, though without effect.'" The story then cites a private letter from someone in Wexford, stating: "'I am sorry to find you are a sufferer in your potato crop. It is the only thing spoken of here. People are justly filled with alarm; but as far as our neighbourhood is concerned, I hear of no remedial measures being adopted, except by a lot of friars here, *who are selling blessed water*, which unfortunate dupes *purchase greedily to sprinkle over their fields.*"'

Given the force of anti-Catholic feeling among Protestants at this time, it would hardly be surprising if this were just a convenient myth, used to bolster the general Protestant sense of Catholicism as a hopelessly superstitious and indeed corrupt form of Christianity. The way the story shifts ground across Longford County might support this view. Indeed, the location had shifted again a few weeks later, when on 20 November *The Times's* Ireland correspondent cited claims that in Lisnaskea, County Fermanagh a priest had 'given a charm of some mixture of holy water' to cure the potatoes.

But it is worth bearing in mind that Catholicism in general hardly discouraged the faithful from believing in magic, given the ability of any priest to routinely turn wine into the blood of Christ. It has been credibly claimed by historians that in Catholic countries ordinary people routinely smuggled mass wafers out of church to put on their crops, in good times as well as during famines. In 1920 one folklorist quoted a discussion between a priest and an old man of eighty one:

'"Why don't you spray your potatoes?"

"I do", said he, "but I don't hold with the Department [of Agriculture]'s spraying. Every St John's Eve for the last fifty years I've sprayed my potatoes with holy water and plenty of it, and it's worked well, and why would I be changing now?"'[8]

88. When Your Number's Up...
The Graphic, 25 December 1851.

'Many of our readers may remember the curious case of a very old woman who destroyed herself under the belief that the Almighty had forgotten to call her out of the world. A native of Bangalore, in the East Indies, who is believed to have reached the age of 135, thought that he had lived long enough, and determined the other day to be buried alive. He announced that he intended the act as a sacrifice to the gods, who, during his long career as a priest, had used him kindly, if not too well. His friends appreciated his generous feeling, and entered eagerly into his views. So the grave was dug, and all arrangements made. Many thousands of admiring and applauding natives assembled to witness the immolation; occupying the trees round about, and every roof in the vicinity, in order to see the end of the holy man. The pious work would inevitably have been accomplished but for the interference, at the last moment, of the British authorities. On the morning of the day named – the 9th October "from information received" – Captain Gompertz, the cantonment magistrate, Dr Orr, the President of the Municipal Board, and the Superintendent of Police, made their way to the village, and put a stop to the intended sacrifice. There was much disappointment among the spectators, who were greatly discontented at being deprived of so interesting a sight; but authority was too strong, and there seemed nothing for it but to disperse.

But the saint announced that he should die some time that day, notwithstanding the prohibition; so the majority of the assemblage waited to see the result. During the day the old man did indeed die, and at eight o'clock in the evening he was buried, with due ceremony, in the grave that had been dug for his living body. He will now become a divinity, at whose shrine reverent villagers will make their simple offerings. And all this took place close to a large city, where half a score of missionaries have been hard at work for more than thirty years.'

89. Divine Revelation.
The Standard, 20 January 1858.

From *The Echo de la Frontieres*, Valenciennes: 'A family named Brisson, consisting of two brothers, one married, two sisters, and a child five years of age, were, a few evenings ago, quietly seated at supper. All at once, one of them, seized with some sudden vertigo, jumped up and began talking most incoherently, and all the other members of the family being attacked in a similar way, did the same. Then they all began dancing, and afterwards stripped themselves of the whole of their garments, singing, as they did so, sacred hymns. They next took the child, stripped him, tied him to a ladder as if to crucify him, and then stuck pins in the fleshy part of his person, continuing to dance and sing all the while. Their next exploit was to ascend to the roof of the house and pour water down the chimney to extinguish, as they said, the fires of purgatory. At this moment the neighbours interfered, and released the little boy, who was insensible from his sufferings. The cause of the sudden madness has not been ascertained.'

90. The Devil's Evening Commute.

Hull Packet and East Riding Times, 22 May 1863.

'At the Hampstead Police Court, on Saturday, Jacob Pattison, a peculiar looking man, with a profusion of long shaggy hair, was charged before Mr J Marshall and Captain Redman with threatening to destroy himself by jumping over the bridge of the Hampstead Heath Tunnel, on the Hampstead Junction railway. Police Constable Daniel Jenkinson ... deposed that a quarter past two in the morning he was on duty in Pond Street, Hampstead, and hearing a noise on the railway bridge he went there, and found the prisoner getting over the parapet. Witness immediately seized him, and asked him what he was doing. The prisoner replied, "Oh, don't touch me; I am the devil, and am going home to hell." Witness, after some difficulty, got him off the bridge, and took him to the Police Station. On the road there the prisoner still persisted in calling himself the devil, that his home was hell, and that the way to it was by jumping off the railway bridge. He further said that if he was not then permitted to do it, he would do so as soon as he could. ... Repeated complaints had been made of his frightening children and young persons by his wild gestures ... Some friends of the prisoner said that if he was discharged they would give an undertaking that he should be looked after. The magistrate discharged the prisoner with a caution.'

91. The Devil on a Rope.
Hampshire Advertiser, 14 October 1865.

'The *Buffalo Courier* states that Mr Leslie having undertaken to give the people of Bayfield, Canada West, a performance on the tightrope, stretched his rope across the James, a distance of 600 feet, and proceeded to walk over it, and, when midway, to go through various manoeuvres and feats of skill. Upon afterwards nearing the opposite bank he found a number of persons greatly excited, and could hear them say, "D—him, he's the devil!" "Cut the rope!", "Cut him down!" etc. Leslie continued to move along on the rope, but before he could reach its terminus, the slender bridge was cut, and he was allowed to fall a distance of nearly 25 feet. In his descent he caught hold of a tree, and thence rolled down the embankment to the water's edge. Finding that he was pursued by the ruffians, he made his escape to the woods, and after travelling about a mile and a half he managed to get a horse and buggy, with which he reached Seaforth.'

92. Just in time for Christmas...
Hampshire Advertiser, 23 December 1865.

'In a sale at Messers Puttick and Simpson's, Leicester Square, on Monday, was a lot (No. 1051) thus described: "a portion of the veil of the Blessed Virgin Mary, inclosed in a small silver reliquary; also a document, under the seal and signature of the Pope's secretary, authenticating the relic." It sold for £4'.

93. Satan's Fund-Raiser.
Hampshire Telegraph, 19 March 1881.

'The Devil in Person.
The other morning, in one of the more frequented thoroughfares of Cracow, the passers-by were surprised to see a genuine devil with horns and tail complete escorted by a gendarme. A closer scrutiny of the interesting stranger led some of them to recognise the maire of a village in the environs. Further inquiries disclosed the reason of his strange disguise.

It seems that in the village of which he was maire a lone peasant woman had lately gained in what is known as the "little lottery" 300 florins, which sum the maire thought would be much better in his own pocket. Dressing himself up in approved diabolical costume, he presented himself to the peasant woman at the witching hour of midnight, and, in a tone of voice suited to his appearance informed her that all money gained in the "little lottery" belonged to his Satanic majesty, to be employed in the destruction of human souls. The woman, frightened to death, at once handed over 75 florins, and confessed that she had deposited 200 more in the savings bank at Cracow. She was enjoined under terrible threats to withdraw and have it ready within 24 hours. The fact of her withdrawing a sum which she had only just deposited piqued the curiosity of the savings bank official, who, with considerable difficulty, extracted from her the story of her nocturnal visitor. The money was handed over to her, but private information was communicated to the police, into whose hands the poor devil of a maire unsuspectingly fell.'

94. Exorcism.
The North Eastern Daily Gazette, 29 December 1886.

'A terrible crime has just been committed in the Morbihan. A miller woman, named Jallu, had four children, two sons, and two daughters. The eldest, Esther Jallu, was pretty, and conscious of the fact. She had also some education, and was a great favourite in the village, where the other inmates of the mill were disliked and feared. One day her family began to affirm that she was possessed of the demon of pride. There was an evil spirit in Esther's body, and the brothers Jallu declared to everybody that they would in some way drive it out.

After ruminating on the matter for some time they barred the doors of the mill, and seizing upon their sister, threw her on the floor. One of them held her down while the other bored holes in her with an augur. The demon was to escape out of her body by these openings. While the screams of the tortured girl were half-drowned by the noise of the mill-stones turning rapidly, two women – the mother and sister – were actually kneeling beside her praying for the success of the operation. Four holes were bored, one in the forehead, one in the body, and one in each leg. Whether these ignorant peasants really imagined that they could thus drive the demon of pride out of their sister, or whether they premeditated the murder they committed, mattered very little for Esther, who, of course, died under the operation. When the inhabitants of the surrounding country came to enquire after Esther, when she had not been seen for several days, the two brothers and the sister appeared at the door armed with hatchets, and threatened to strike anyone who should dare to approach them. The gendarmes were at once informed of the occurrence, and the inmates of the mill having been seized, they were sent to a madhouse'.

95. A Sicilian Pilgrimage.

The Star, 24 February 1891.

'The British Consul at Messina mentions a characteristic example of a Sicilian pilgrimage. At a mountain town about fifty miles from Messina there is a festa in September called the Madonna of the Chain (Madonna della Catena). If a man is dangerously ill, or in trouble, or in love, or for whatever reason it may be, he vows to go for one, two, three, or four years on the pilgrimage of the "Madonna della Catena". The devotees strip themselves of all but a cloth about their loins. They have in their hands soft pieces of pithy wood, called *sferza*, about the diameter of a penny piece, through which are stuck from forty to fifty pins, their points projecting one-eighth of an inch. The procession starts from the town to the chapel of the Madonna della Catena, about four miles distant; the men stab themselves with these pins on the shoulders, breast, thighs and legs, shouting all the time, the women encouraging them with wine and bread, and the priest leads the way with a banner.

When the Vice Consul saw this there were over 100 men in the procession, and the stabs given over and over again on the same spots caused horrible bleeding tumours, and two deaths occurred. The women who have made vows pass their tongues along the ground through every impurity from the church door to the high altar. The men, it is said, never break a vow when made under the sense of religion'.

The Unexplained, and the Uncategorisable

Readers may well be forgiven for mentally categorising some of these tales under previous chapter headings. All I can say is, if one thing seems to unite these gems from our strange century, it is this: you really could not make them up.

96. Untitled...
The Times, 4 April 1844.

'The *Honfleur Journal*, after noticing that for some time the Chalet, or Swiss Cottage, of Monsieur Guttinguer, at St Gatien, on the skirts of the forest of Pennedepie, had been disturbed by strange and unaccountable noises, which the country people attributed to a ghost, goes on to say... "On Tuesday last knockings were heard at the doors of all the apartments of the house; and, though they had been locked by the man in charge, were all found open in the morning. On Wednesday, a decorator employed at the Chalet, and intending to sleep there, having no faith in ghosts, locked all the doors himself, and took the keys into his own room. During the night, the watchman called him up to show him the ghost, and, in fact, he saw in an outer gallery, a figure all in white, resembling a camel, making motions with its head. The watchman fired upon the apparition, which immediately leaped down from the gallery, uttering cries which were not those, which a camel or any other animal, brute or human, was likely to make. The decorator would have pursued the discomfited spectre, but was prevented by the necessity of attending to two women in the house, who had fainted from affright, and before he was at liberty the nocturnal visitor had disappeared. On examining the rooms, all the doors were found wide open; the carpets had been rolled up, and, with the chair covers, thrown out on the staircase. The watchman also became ill, complaining that he had received a violent blow on the chest while levelling his gun at the ghost; but we imagine it was from the recoil of his own piece. Since that night no supernatural object has been seen about the place".

97. 'Roman Superstition and Cruelty'.

Daily News, 29 January 1858.

From our own correspondent – Rome, Jan 23.

'Although the science of demonology and the practice of witchcraft are nearly abolished in countries boasting of Christian civilisation, or but faintly represented by the modern accomplishments of table-turning or spirit-rapping, some lingering remains of the black art, in its legitimate mediaeval darkness, are occasionally brought before the notice of the ecclesiastical authorities in this country, more specially those appointed to take cognisance of such mysterious matters, by whom their authors are rigorously prosecuted as guilty of *fattucchieirie* and *stregonerie* (sorcery and witch-craft). A striking and almost incredible example of the invocation of diabolic aid, under circumstances which betray a great degree of avarice and cruelty, has recently occurred on the shores of the Adriatic in the province of La Marea.

A Lady of some property residing generally at Acqua Santa in the Papal dominions, but bordering on the Neapolitan territory, in which she also has property, has become possessed with the strongest conviction that in some part of her estates there is a hidden treasure of enormous value, but that all her attempts at its discovery are systematically opposed by evil spirits. Having been informed by some trustworthy old woman, who bears the reputation of being a *strega*, or witch, that nothing can allay the spite of these hostile spirits, and lead to the discovery of the treasure, except sacrificing to them a male child of good parentage and under 6 years of age, this treasure-seeking signora has been for some months in quest of a child adapted for her purpose, and not too closely guarded for her kidnapping intentions.

About a month ago she cast her evil eye upon a fine little boy belonging to an English Lady residing at Porto di Fermo, and skilfully watching her opportunity, contrived to entice the child away whilst rambling with its mother, and playing about on the seashore. The consternation of the mother at the child's disappearance may be easily imagined. Her husband being absent from home at the time, she sent a young man, her son-in-law, in quest of the child, and of the treasure-seeker who had inveigled him away. Towards night the young man succeeded in tracing the fugitive to a solitary house at a considerable distance, into which he endeavoured to obtain admittance, but was repulsed by the hostile demonstrations of a body of armed retainers. He then proceeded to the neighbouring town of Ascoli to procure the assistance of the police, with a sufficient force of whom he returned to the solitary house, but too late to arrest the kidnappers, who had decamped with their victim. Meanwhile, the father of the child returned to his home, and having learnt of the catastrophe, came out likewise in hot pursuit, which resulted, after several days' research, in the discovery of the hiding place of the lady and child, at a curate's house in the Neapolitan dominions.

During this interval the Lady's house at Acqua Santa was subjected to a judicial search, and evidence was obtained that the child was to have been sacrificed there on Christmas day. An altar had been prepared, with wax torches and all kind of accessories, to immolate the boy to Satan! An ambuscade was established around the dwelling in consequence of this horrible revelation, and a party kept constantly on the watch, in case the lady should return to her habitual residence.

In the meantime the father, having come up with the fugitives, demanded his child from the curate who harboured them; but the priest refused to comply, except on condition of a full pardon to the lady. Unwilling to pass over so heinous a transaction, the infuriated father appealed without delay to the bishop of the diocese, who took instant measures to rescue the child, and to arrest the lady, who is now undergoing a trial for *stregoneria*, or witch-craft, and will most likely be punished accordingly.

The Pope takes the greatest interest in the proceedings, and is punctually informed of every point of interest developed by the examination. The child was absent from home about five days, during which time the mother nearly lost her senses, and has yet hardly recovered her tranquility. She is the sister of an English gentleman, who has for many years been engaged in one of the banking establishments of Rome.'

98. Human Hibernation?
Leeds Mercury, 29 July 1893.
'Buried Alive by his Own Wish'.

'It appears that the authorities in Chicago are going to allow Seymour, the thought-reader, to carry out his extraordinary scheme of being buried alive and remaining underground long enough for a crop of barley to be grown on his grave. The coffin is made in three sections, one fitting inside the other. In it Seymour is to be buried six feet deep. The barley is to be sown on the grave immediately after the burial, and he calculates that on Sept 24th it will have had time to grow, ripen, and be reaped. Signals are to be arranged by means of which he can communicate with the soldiers guarding the grave, should anything go wrong. The general impression seems to be that if Seymour carries out his plan of being buried alive, he will probably remain underground for good.'

Newcastle Weekly Courant, 12 August 1893.

'In America a "crank" named Seymour is about to undergo the experiment of being buried alive, with a view of surviving the ordeal. For several days prior to being put in his grave he will be fed on fat heat-producing fluid; he will then throw himself into a cataleptic state, his lungs being filled with pure air to their fullest capacity. The mouth, nose, ears, and eyes will be hermetically sealed, and after this paraffin will be spread over the entire body to close the pores. Seymour will then be placed in a casket of longer size than the ordinary coffin, and that again will be laid inside another casket. Both will be perforated, so that any gases escaping from the body will be absorbed by the soil in which the interment will be made. The man will be allowed to remain in the ground for eighteen days. The probability is that when he is taken from the grave at the end of his probation there will be an inquest.'

The Belfast Newsletter, 26 August 1893.

Two weeks later the *British Medical Journal* cited with great scepticism claims of Indian fakirs having done this: 'in some instances the grave in which the devotee has proposed to hibernate has been uncovered after the lapse of a few days and its occupant found dead. When, therefore, we are told that Seymour, the thought-reader, proposes at Chicago to be buried alive and "remain underground long enough for a crop of barley to be grown on his grave" we incline to share the general impression that if he carries out his plan "he will probably remain underground for good".'

With this story running and running on both sides of the Atlantic, the Indian fakirs were not the only parallels which came to light...

Hampshire Telegraph, 2 September 1893.

'The stoppage of the heart's beating is not regarded as a satisfactory evidence of death. In some cases on record that organ has apparently ceased to perform its function for as much as fifteen minutes, yet the person has revived. Tidey, the great English authority, speaks of the instance of a certain Colonel Townshend, who was seemingly able to die at will, and to come to life again when he chose. On a number of occasions he had deliberately suspended his own vital processes for a short time. Finally, he consulted physicians on the subject, deeming his ability to do this a sufficiently abnormal symptom to be somewhat alarming. In the presence of the doctors he voluntarily lapsed into a state of torpidity, his heart stopped, and his breathing also, a mirror held at his mouth showing no dimness.'

The case was apparently unique. At the same time the peculiar faculty developed by Colonel Townshend – who died the same night for good and all – bears a seeming likeness to the peculiar power exhibited by certain fakirs of India.

For centuries it has been a familiar trick for certain of these fakirs who possessed the accomplishment to permit themselves to be buried alive for months, coming to life again after being dug up. That the remarkable feat is wholly bona fide has been satisfactorily demonstrated.

It has been repeatedly performed in the presence of most sceptical witnesses, under circumstances which preclude all possibility of deception. It is an artificial suspension of vitality, bearing some relation to the natural hibernation of bats and other animals.'

Townshend's abilities do seem to have been genuine. They are described in the medical work, *The English Malady* (1733), by physician George Cheyne, who, along with other eminent doctors, watched the Colonel perform this feat, and after very careful examination concluded that he had in fact killed himself by mistake. Shortly after, Townshend revived. That said, this was the early eighteenth century – a time when a surprising number of people, rich and poor, were mistakenly buried alive. After spending some time wondering about Seymour's supposed ability, I sent these stories over to Michael Bell, American folklorist and author of the vampire book *Food for the Dead*. Michael rummaged up some US stories on Seymour's plan, concluding that the whole thing was a stunt designed to attract audiences to Seymour's other magical performances.

Rockford Spectator, 7 July 1893.

'An old showman said: "Seymour is a sleight of hand fakir and has been working a rich graft in the little towns. That bit in the paper this morning is only advance work and the next you'll hear will be that he has hired the Auditorium or the Columbia or some other theatre for a farewell show just before he gets buried. As soon as he gets the money from a big audience he'll give his show and conclude that life os worth living for a little longer. He's a smooth one. Bury himself six feet under ground? Not in a thousand years. It's all an advertising bluff.'

The chronology below shows us how slowly local news could travel in the nineteenth century, with the *New York Times* being well behind the times, a week after Rockford readers abandoned their hopes of watching barley grow over Seymour's grave.

Cleveland Plain Dealer, 16 September 16, 1893.

'Seymour, the mind reader, says he has given up the idea of being buried alive and waiting to be dug up until a crop of oats sown on his grave is harvested. He was threatened with prosecution for attempting suicide if he survived, and the choice between staying dead and going to prison was not to his liking, so he decided to remain above ground and sow his wild oats somewhere else than on his grave.'

New York Times, 9 September 1893.
'Will someone please bury me?'

'Andrew J. Seymour, the Western mind-reader, arrived in this city yesterday with his son and daughter, and registered at the Hoffman House. He intends to place his children in school in the East. Then he will do one of two things: take a trip to Europe or bury himself. It depends somewhat upon the weather.

Mr Seymour is tall, pleasant-looking, and middle-aged. He has recently acquired fame in a novel way. He announced that he could suspend animation for ninety days, and requested of the public, as a personal favour, that they would bury him six feet under ground in a nice hardwood coffin with silver handles. This done, the public would greatly oblige by planting a small crop of No.1 assorted red eye wheat on his grave.

When the sun had ripened the wheat it should be cut and stored away. Then Mr Seymour would be dug up and come out of it all with a cheerful smile on his western countenance.

This was to be done at the World's Fair in August, but Major Carter Harrison said he didn't want live people burying themselves in his town. The experiment might be successful; he had heard that it was in India, but a live man was better than a dead scientific experiment.

"I was deeply disappointed", said Mr Seymour ... and so was my associate, Dr E.C. Dunn of Rockford. This thing is simple enough. It has been done successfully in India, and there is no reason why I shouldn't do it. Why, five years ago I voluntarily suspended animation for twenty one days. I made it a condition that I should not be disturbed until the full time had elapsed, as such action might prove fatal. Then I "willed" myself to sleep and woke up on time, just as I had mentally agreed to. I needed the rest, too, as I had been working very hard. I intend to be buried for ninety days, at Rockford, Illinois, if I can get a burial permit. There's the difficulty. The authorities heretofore have refused me burial permits. I may have to erect a mound and go to sleep, so to speak, on top of that, if burial is denied. Of course, if cold weather sets in, I shall be compelled to defer my experiment until Spring. In that case I shall spend the Winter abroad."

Rockford Morning Star, 22 September 1893.

'A.J. Seymour, the Rockford crank who was advertised to be buried alive, has changed his mind, as every one knew he would, and says the authorities of the state would not allow him to perform this fool act'.

99. Burning the Devil Out.
Cheshire Observer, 1 April 1893.

The *Frankfurter Zeitung* reports an extraordinary instance of superstition in Italy. At Pontea Ema, near Florence, lives a peasant whose daughter is suffering from a bad form of hysteria, going about the house screaming the whole night, and frightening all with her hallucinations. The priest of the place stated that the girl was possessed of a devil. Masses were said, but these were of no avail, and it was stated that her case was one to be cured only by a person versed in exorcising evil spirits. [The father] must go to the Via Pitti, near Florence, where, he was told, lived a famous sorceress.

The peasant and his daughter went there. Arrived at the house in the Via Pitti, the peasant knocked; an old woman appeared at the door. "Are you the wise woman?" said he. On receiving a reply in the affirmative, and being ushered into a room, in which two wax candles were burning, he laid his case before her, finishing with, 'my daughter is bewitched, and can only be cured, I am told, by someone skilled in witchcraft." The wise woman said she dealt with such cases. Her usual charge for driving out an ordinary devil was five lira; for exorcising Beelzebub was twenty five lira. The peasant therefore counted out twenty five lira. The house was in darkness. The old woman told her guests to follow her, and to kneel down in every room they entered. The howling that went on in every room was truly dreadful. The peasant and his daughter were filled with confidence. "You two", said the old woman, "have only to return home and set light to your oven fire. The first person who knocks at your door is the cause of your daughter's sickness. Therefore", said she, turning to the peasant, "as soon as anyone crosses your threshold, seize and place that person, in the presence of your daughter, in the oven."

With this advice the pair went home, and the peasant kindled a fire as the woman directed. The fire was kept up the whole night, but no one knocked. At the break of day a knock was heard. "Who is there?" asked the peasant. "For heaven's sake give me a piece of bread", said the voice without. The peasant opened the door, and saw in front of him a poor old woman, trembling with cold and hunger. Without any further ado he caught her up in his arms, and placed her in the oven. The cries of the poor creature were dreadful to hear. Fortunately some milkmen happened to be passing, and they burst open the door, when the woman, more dead than alive, was taken out of the oven. The actors in this shocking drama are in the hands of justice.'

Although the custom of April Fools Day had been running for many decades by this point, readers can be assured that this story had first appeared on 29 March, and was no hoax. Notice, here, the implicit connivance of the priest, which mirrors that of the curate in the Italian child sacrifice affair of 1858.

100. "Letters from Heaven".
Reynolds's Newspaper, 23 October 1898.

'A trial which has just taken place at the Bavarian country town of Kempten, the centre of an almost purely Roman Catholic population, reveals the existence of such extraordinary ignorance and superstition that the details are worth noticing, writes the Vienna correspondent of the Daily News.

A married couple at Kaufbeuern, Alois and Rosine Wolhfahrt, lived in extreme poverty, shared by the illegitimate daughter of the wife, a girl of 18 named Agnes, who suffered from an incurable disease. The family had lived for years on money obtained by touching letters written by the invalid.

BEGINNING THE DECEPTION

In 1893 an old schoolfellow of the girl, Cecilia Kottrich, began to visit her, and, moved to pity by the poverty of the sick girl, prevailed upon her own parents, who are well-to-do farmers, to give their assistance. She was thenceforth allowed to take Agnes her dinner every day and a mark or two every week for little extras.

After some time Agnes confided to her young friend Cecilia that the Virgin Mary often appeared to her and that she was in correspondence with her and also with Crescence, Cecilia's sister, who had died a year previously, and who had also been their schoolfellow. Agnes whispered the secret that Crescence was not in heaven but in purgatory.

BLEEDING THE FAMILY

These mystic communications affected Cecilia's health, and she began to suffer from hysterical attacks. Agnes, no doubt inspired by her needy mother, always on the look-out for crooked ways by which she could obtain money, proposed that when the Virgin Mary next appeared to her, she would ask her to let her take Cecilia's sufferings upon herself.

By the time Cecilia came again the Virgin had consented, but Cecilia's parents must make a sacrifice and pay 200 marks. They did this willingly, and from that time forward during three years the "messages from heaven" never ceased.

The Virgin herself proposed that Crescence should be delivered from purgatory. 300 marks were all that was needed. Farmer Kottrich paid the sum.

HAD MARRIED AN ANGEL

A little later the news came from heaven that Crescence had married an angel – she wished to have her dowry sent, and 1000 marks for furnishing her new home. Then after a time came the news that Crescence, who was very happy, had given birth to a child. Would they send money for the wants of the baby?

By this time Cecilia had no more attacks, and Farmer Kottrich and his wife believed it was "all right".

LETTERS FROM HEAVEN

At the trial the Kottriches produced 52 letters which Agnes had transmitted from heaven, and these were not all, some being lost. Every sheet of paper had the picture of a saint upon it. Those from the Virgin Mary had a gilt edge. Imagine the sensation in Court when the Public Prosecutor read a receipt "from the Mother of Christ" for 150 marks; and a request for a higher amount, signed, "In heavenly glory, Joseph and Mary".

A letter expressing thanks for money received and for excellent potatoes; another announcing the receipt of 2,000 marks, signed "daughter, son-in-law, and little baby", with the remark added that when the money arrived "all the angels in heaven blew their trumpets".

AND SOME FURNITURE

Perhaps the most remarkable fact of all is that "Our Lady" and "Sister Crescence" sent their dear ones some things from heaven, from "the heavenly hall" – a sofa, a large milk loaf, pieces of clothing, a silver watch, and a gold ring, but this last had to be returned after a short time.

Frau Kottrich herself baked a fine tart for the Virgin Mary.

TWO YEARS IMPRISONMENT

The mother denied all knowledge of the affair, but she was found "Guilty" and was sentenced to two years' imprisonment. Her husband, who is too stupid to have helped in the deceit, was sentenced to two months' imprisonment for receiving stolen goods.'

Amen.

[1] www.oldbaileyonline.org (t18040111-79).

[2] For more on this remarkable event, see: S. J. Connolly, 'The "Blessed Turf": Cholera and Popular Panic in Ireland, June 1832', *Irish Historical Studies* 23.91 (1983): 214-232.

[3] Susan Schoon Eberly, 'Fairies and the Folklore of Disability: Changelings, Hybrids and the Solitary Fairy' *Folklore* 99.1 (1988): 58-77.

[4] http://www.victorianweb.org/economics/wages.html

[5] Country Antrim Folklore Today', *Ulster Journal of Archaeology* 1 (1938): 208-214, 209; 'Witch-rabbits in Devonshire', *Folklore*, 68.1 (1957): 296.

[6] *Five Godly and Profitable Sermons* (1628), 17-18.

[7] *Lightning As A 'Photographer': Revisiting a Forgotten Phenomenon of Nature* (Createspace, 2013).
http://mattweeks.hubpages.com/hub/The-Lightning-Portrait-of-the-Pickens-County-Courthouse#

[8] Mrs John Borland, 'Some Kerry Notes', *Folklore* 31.3 (1920): 234-237, 235.

Many thanks to Michael Bell and Steve Schlozman for friendly advance reading.

Printed in Great Britain
by Amazon